Suicidal Behaviour

Suicidal Behaviour

BY

J. WALLACE McCULLOCH

AND

ALISTAIR E. PHILIP

PERGAMON PRESS

OXFORD · NEW YORK · TORONTO
SYDNEY · BRAUNSCHWEIG

Pergamon Press Ltd., Headington Hill Hall, Oxford
Pergamon Press Inc., Maxwell House, Fairview Park, Elmsford,
New York 10523
Pergamon of Canada Ltd., 207 Queen's Quay West, Toronto 1
Pergamon Press (Aust.) Pty. Ltd., 19a Boundary Street,
Rushcutters Bay, N.S.W. 2011, Australia
Vieweg & Sohn GmbH, Burgplatz 1, Braunschweig

First edition 1972
Reprinted 1973

Library of Congress Catalog Card No. 72–188140

Printed in Great Britain by The Anchor Press Ltd., Tiptree, Essex

08 016855 8

To

SARAH AND BETTY

for numerous late homecomings

Is there for honest poverty,
That hangs his head and a' that;
The coward-slave, we pass him by,
We dare be poor for a' that!
For a' that, and a' that,
Our toil's obscure, and a' that;
The rank is but the guinea's stamp,
The man's the gowd for a' that.

ROBERT BURNS

Contents

Editor's Foreword

THIS book is a welcome addition to the Pergamon Social Work Division and is addressed to those who may become "helpers" in the face of clients' or patients' potential or actual suicide. It should be useful to those working in the newly formed social service departments, the psychiatric hospitals or the voluntary services such as the Samaritans, as well as to a wider group in the field of medicine. The authors have between them worked in a professional capacity—one as a social worker and the other as a clinical psychologist—with people who have demonstrated the whole range of suicidal behaviour. The book draws on this experience and it also reflects their ability as teachers to conceptualize from the fields of sociology, psychology and individual psychopathology. It is hoped that this book will be put to *use* and help directly those troubled people who turn their aggression on themselves.

JEAN P. NURSTEN

Acknowledgements

MUCH of the work reported in this book was carried out while both authors were members of the Medical Research Council Unit for Research on the Epidemiology of Psychiatric Illness. We are grateful to all our former colleagues for their criticisms and encouraging comments. We owe a special debt of gratitude to all the staff of the Poisoning Treatment Centre of the Royal Infirmary of Edinburgh—it is just possible that our efforts will reduce the need for their existence.

Thanks are due to G. A. Foulds & Tavistock Publications Ltd. for permission to quote two paragraphs from *Personality and Personal Illness*, to the World Health Organization for permission to use their Table 11 from their monograph *Prevention of Suicide*, and to Mrs. Joyce Scott, who typed the manuscript.

Introduction

The Magnitude of the Problem

Suicide is a problem which confronts all members of the community, but especially those in the "helping" professions. It is imperative that the student of social work or medicine, and also interested lay bodies like the Samaritans, learn the facts about suicidal behaviour in all its forms. It is important to allay students' fears about suicidal behaviour and equally important to correct popular misconceptions. Very early in their own practice or clinical training, to say nothing of their own social circle, students will find themselves confronted with behaviour which ranges from the so-called *gesture* to a completed fatal act. The threat of suicide can be even more anxiety provoking than the threat of murder. One can flee or oppose the latter but the former cannot be resolved so simply.

This might sound dramatic, but mistakes made in response to a cry for help can have serious consequences. The aim of this book is to try to provide such knowledge of the subject that the reader will be able to *hear* a cry for help and to respond to it in a manner appropriate to his skills. Suicidal behaviour in its fatal and non-fatal manifestations is a social and medical problem which is much more common than might be anticipated. It is difficult to comprehend the fact that in the world, every year, the equivalent of the population of a city such as Edinburgh or Helsinki kills itself. In addition, in the same period of time, the equivalent of the population of London indulges in some form of non-fatal suicidal behaviour.

In more precise terms, the world death rate by suicide averages out at 13 persons in every 100,000 each year. Non-fatal acts, while impossible to tabulate accurately, must be manifested by upwards of 120 persons per 100,000 annually. These figures are minimal, and to them must be added an unknown proportion of events which are classed as accidental poisonings,

1

road accidents, and other untimely occurrences. Imperfect though these figures may be, it is possible for the reader to have some comprehension of the problem by considering data concerning the United Kingdom.

Although with a death rate of some 13 per 100,000 suicide contributes far fewer deaths than illnesses such as cancer or coronary heart disease, whose rates are about 210 and 250 per 100,000, it is, nevertheless, a cause for concern. The concern is all the greater since suicide is considered to be caused by social and psychological rather than physiological factors. Rationally or not, we all feel that these former factors should be more amenable to identification, prevention and treatment than they are at present. The fact that we feel this way, while also feeling anxious and inadequate, may to some extent account for the fact that suicidal behaviour, especially completed suicide, tends to be ignored as a public health or social action problem by all but a few bodies. It seems anomalous that deaths by suicide should be so treated, while road fatalities, which account for approximately the same number of deaths per year, are combated by publicity campaigns and legislation which attempt to change people's attitudes and behaviour.

It is strange that road deaths, where the human factor looms no larger than it does in suicide and where in some cases there are suicidal connotations, strike people as being untimely and avoidable while these sentiments are felt less often about suicide and other major forms of disease.

While not wishing to dwell on things statistical or to focus attention on completed suicide, throughout the book recourse will be made to statistical data which will be presented as simply as possible. Many writers on this subject have been tempted to make international comparisons of official suicide rates. An example of a comparison using official rates is that of Sainsbury and Barraclough,* who have shown rates which vary between 2 and 25 persons per 100,000. Kessel has made a study where the differences mentioned have been taken into account and has shown that although Danish rates for completed suicide are $1\frac{1}{2}$ times greater than those for England and Wales, "Comparison of decisions made by coroners in Britain and medical examiners in Denmark on the same sets of data indicate that a sizeable proportion of the differences in suicide rates for the two countries could be explained on the basis of decision making practised by the responsible authorities." Even within a country like Great Britain, where public records are as sophisticated as anywhere in the world, the

* Detailed references to papers and books are contained in the Bibliography (p. 111).

suicide rate varies between the constituent countries and even within regions. Northern Ireland has a rate which is half that of England, while Scotland and Wales have rates which fall between these extremes. It is known, for instance, that the attitude of the law to suicidal acts has varied very substantially over the years between England and Scotland, being punitive in the former and tending towards indifference in the latter. This must have affected the reporting of such acts. Similarly, differences in religion and other social attitudes lead to different reported rates for suicidal behaviour. Because of these difficulties in collating and comparing international and even intranational rates we make no apology for drawing heavily on our clinical experience and our research studies, which cover all aspects of suicidal behaviour occurring in the city of Edinburgh. We know of no other city where one ward of one hospital handles the majority of known cases of self-poisoning or self-injury, and where an experienced medico-psychiatric team attempts to determine the motive and intention of each act. This ward, the Poisoning Treatment Centre of the Royal Infirmary of Edinburgh, deals with cases of poisoning in the city, and therefore the *accidental* category is minimal. All adults who have deliberately poisoned or injured themselves in any part of the city or its immediate environs can be sent to this unit. If they are first taken to another hospital it is usual for them to be transferred, but the great majority are brought directly to the Infirmary, where it is the practice to send to the unit all patients who have taken an overdose or who have injured themselves, regardless of the severity of the wound or the number of tablets which have been ingested. Every case is accepted. It is true that occasionally a patient admitted to another hospital may discharge himself before he can be transferred, but investigations have shown that the basic characteristics of those who are not transferred are similar to those who are. Before the toxicological skills of the physician were augmented by social and psychiatric investigation, many old people were admitted, treated and discharged as "accidental coal-gas poisoning". Explanations such as "the kettle boiled over and put the gas out" were accepted at face value. It is obvious that some of these people were returned home while still at risk and whose next attempt might prove fatal. Social malaise and personal psychopathology are reflected in attempts at suicide; these problems are emphasized by the fact that one-quarter of admissions to the Poisoning Treatment Centre have made a previous attempt. Further, it has been found that at least 1 person in every 4 completed suicides occurring in the city had made a previous attempt to kill himself. It is very clear that people who attempt suicide are very much at risk of killing themselves at a later date. From its relation to suicide and from the social and personal distress it both causes and reflects, attempted suicide is a public health problem of great magnitude.

The Problem of Nomenclature

For suicidal behaviour of all types we have amassed a wealth of social, psychiatric and psychological information. The problem of nomenclature in studies of attempted suicide has led to imprecision, but it is generally agreed that the existing term *attempted suicide* is unsatisfactory, for the reason that many patients so designated are not trying to kill themselves. At popular and professional levels this state of affairs has led to notions such as suicidal gestures, failed suicide, pseudocide, parasuicide and the like. The main objection to categorizing people as attempted suicides is that such an interpretation of a piece of behaviour taken in isolation tends to be made *before* the social and psychological investigations have been initiated. That is to say, when a person presents at a casualty department having taken an overdose, the assumption is often made that the patient has attempted suicide. However, if the patient is ambulant and the dose seems to have been small, an equally erroneous assumption is often made. A diagnosis of "gesture" is recorded and the patient sent on his way. It follows, therefore, that when a person deliberately poisons or injures himself but does not intend to die, he is categorized as an attempted suicide. Such labelling so structures the situation that alternative views of the behaviour become less viable. Kessel has claimed that the term self-poisoning is preferable to attempted suicide, arguing that the former term arouses fewer preconceived notions in the minds of the uninitiated. In situations which might be called crises of despair, some people injure themselves in order to appeal for help, to spite others, or to submit themselves to trial by ordeal. It can be established fairly easily whether or not an overdose was taken deliberately, but it is not as easy to say whether death was intended. Yet all these behaviours are classed as attempted suicide.

Perhaps the most notable contribution to the problem of definition in this field has been that of Shneidman. In his paper entitled "Suicide, sleep and death" he points out that the threat to an individual's life caused by a bullet, a steering wheel or a virulent infection can be classified as homicide, accident or illness, yet to the individual concerned they are all simply threats to life. While it may seem that the process of classification is carried out solely to help the researcher or clinician, it should add to the understanding of the patient's part in the drama. Such classification should help us discover some of the overt or covert ways in which an individual may attempt to facilitate his own death. The aim of any system of classification must not only be to help formulate the problem, it must also cast light on the needs of the patient. In this book we have not dwelled on the problems of formulating a classificatory system. The interested reader may wish to consult some of the source material listed in the Bibliography. For ease of reading we will use the term *attempted suicide*, with all its reservations, throughout the remainder of the book.

The Relationship of Suicide to Attempted Suicide

Many people who kill themselves do so at the first attempt and for this reason are beyond help. Since the aim of this book is to enlighten and to help people prevent suicide, we make no apology for separating suicide from attempted suicide and for placing our emphasis on the latter. For this reason discussion of suicide will feature less prominently.

Although attempted suicide and suicide can profitably be considered independently, it is worth bearing in mind again the extent to which the two overlap. Of 216 suicides occurring in Edinburgh between 1963 and 1965, 53 (25 per cent) had a recorded history of at least one previous episode of attempted suicide. Of the 511 persons seen in the Poisoning Treatment Centre during 1962 and 1963 almost 1 in 20 have since died by suicide—a high figure for so comparatively rare an event.

The number of published studies of suicidal behaviour is immense, and a recent bibliography has been produced by the United States Public Health Service which shows that in the 60 years following the publication of Durkheim's systematic sociological study in 1897 just over 2000 contributions to the literature have been made. In the decade following 1957 the flow of articles has trebled. The task of synthesizing the results of such a mass of data is simplified by the fact that the quality and scientific standing of these contributions are varied; speculative, woolly papers lie cheek by jowl with others whose conclusions are cautious and closely related to observed data. Such dissimilarities reflect the wide range of interests, orientations, and training of the many professions involved in studying suicidal behaviour. Few authors have made more than a passing contribution to the body of knowledge, and four centres stand out as having made major contributions in theory, methodology, and experimental findings. Pride of place must go to Farberow and Shneidman of Los Angeles whose prodigious output of fact and theory has led to the rapid development of suicide prevention agencies throughout the United States as well as providing much stimulation to other workers. In Philadelphia, the work of Tuckman and his co-workers has contributed much factual information, especially in relating suicidal behaviour to other indices of social disorder. In the United Kingdom, Stengel has contributed much to our awareness of the magnitude of the problem posed by suicidal behaviour; as with the Los Angeles workers, his theoretical formulations have been as important as his experimental findings.

The Edinburgh centre, fortunate in having a succession of research workers who turned their attention to the problems of suicidal behaviour in general rather than to its manifestations in the limited sphere of the psychiatric hospital, merits a place beside these three, the contributions of Batchelor in the 1950's and Kessel a decade later having been influential and provocative. Research in Edinburgh has highlighted the value of serial studies of suicidal behaviour where one can recognize not only the growing magnitude of the problem but also shifts in orientation and assumption about the population under scrutiny.

CHAPTER 1

Social Findings

BEARING in mind the overlap which has already been mentioned, suicide and attempted suicide show different age and sex patterns. Our Edinburgh figures may be used to demonstrate this. Of the various methods used in all suicidal behaviour there is little evidence to suggest that any one method is more lethal than any other. The use of firearms may be an exception here, but since countries such as the United Kingdom are particularly rigorous in gun-licensing laws, shooting is not a common method in either of the two groups. There are, however, differences of method within each group. That is to say there are relationships between age and method and sex and method.

Age and Sex

Authors are generally agreed that the incidence of *suicide* increases with increasing age. Allowing for true variation and differences of reporting, it is probable that the modal age for both sexes lies somewhere in the late forties, but for each decade thereafter the rate tends to increase. In Edinburgh it was found that the mean age for men who committed suicide was 48 years and that this did not differ significantly from that of the women, whose mean age fell at 51 years. Overall, there was an increasing rate of suicide with increasing age.

For *attempted suicide* the pattern is different. Although there have been fluctuations in the age range for attempted suicide according to sex, attempted suicide is much more practised by young people. The rates for both sexes tend to be highest in the late teens and early twenties, and it is here that the difference between the sexes is most apparent. Recent studies have suggested, however, that young men are now attempting suicide

7

more frequently than hitherto, whereas for women the picture remains unchanged. Unlike completed suicide, there is a progressive decline in the rates of attempted suicide with increasing years, and by the time the late forties are reached there is also parity between the sexes.

In Edinburgh today it has been found that 1 teenager in every 250 deliberately poisons or injures herself every year. This rate is almost double what it was 5 years ago, and at the time of writing no plausible explanations have been proffered. Perhaps we would have to examine in detail the meaning of the alleged "generation gap" to the adolescent and his attitude to life. This is beyond the scope of this book, and, indeed, beyond our comprehension. It has been suggested that self-poisoning is a fashion akin to swooning in Victorian days, and fashions change. It can be concluded that for Edinburgh, at least, there has been a real rise in attempted suicide over all sex age groups, particularly in the case of the young and especially for young men.

Professional thought on suicide in the United Kingdom has largely depended on the work of Sainsbury, who carried out an extensive study of the ecology of suicide in London. His findings (that suicide rates increased with age, particularly among males, and that there was an excess of males at each age group) have had some support from other studies. However, a narrowing of the male–female sex ratio was noted by Stengel and Cook in 1961. This was caused by the male rate remaining constant while that for women increased. This finding has been found to hold good in Edinburgh for the years 1963–5, where parity of the sexes was observed. Unlike most studies of completed suicide, which have stressed its incidence in the elderly, the Edinburgh studies have been able to identify two distinguishable groups of suicides. One appears to follow the classic elderly pattern while the other involves a much younger group, aged between 25 and 34 years of age. We tentatively suggest that this latter group represents a spill-over from the attempted suicide group; this will be discussed later from several viewpoints. It is tempting to ascribe the rising female suicide rate, which has parallels in certain other ailments such as lung cancer and coronary heart disease, to the changing role of women in our society. In order to test this hypothesis, however, we would have to demonstrate that "emancipated" women have contributed disproportionately to the rise in the female rates, and this we are unable to do.

More and more we find that suicidal behaviour involves the use of drugs given for therapeutic reasons, and in consequence most of our findings on the methods used in attempted suicide will be dealt with in Chapter 2, which deals with the psychiatric aspects of the problem. However, it is noted in passing that there are differences in method as it relates both to age and fatality. It must also be remembered that method is related to "availability" and this, too, will be discussed later. In America it has been found that there has been a remarkable alteration in the methods used in suicidal acts in the past decade. There the use of drugs in suicide has increased to a disproportionate extent while other means have generally fallen out of favour. The increase in drugs is due not to the widely prescribed non-barbiturate sedative and tranquillizing drugs, as might be thought, but entirely to the prescription of barbiturates, which accounts for 75 per cent of all *suicides* caused by the ingestion of drugs. It also represents by far the largest percentage of suicide where the drugs used have been prescribed by doctors. Firearms and hanging, although still far more common in the United States than in the United Kingdom, do not show the same rapid increase shown by drugs. Of course, the ready availability of firearms in the United States is unparalleled anywhere else in the world, so it is to be expected that such a readily available, lethal method should feature more highly there than elsewhere. Over the same decade in Edinburgh drugs accounted for more than 50 per cent of all completed suicides, with coal-gas poisoning coming a close second. Surprisingly, coal-gas poisoning was not the most commonly used method by the elderly and lonely as might be expected from the popular notion of the suicide act. It was, in fact, a statistically significant finding that gas was a method most favoured by the 15-to-34-year-old group. Older people showed no excess of any one method over any other.

The picture for *attempted suicide* is somewhat different where coal-gas and aspirin are clearly age-related methods. The use of coal-gas in attempts rises proportionately with age, while the ingestion of aspirin shows a peak in the teens and then falls dramatically. While less marked, the use of barbiturates also increases with increased age, but for all other drugs age is of little importance.

It has already been indicated that the number of cases admitted to the Poisoning Treatment Centre in Edinburgh has increased steadily over the past few years, and it is noteworthy that this increase has been paralleled in other areas of Britain. Although the number of teenagers involved in this dangerous behaviour has increased dramatically over the past decade, their use of salicilates (e.g. aspirin) has remained remarkably constant. Presumably, young people take this kind of drug because it is often less easy for them to obtain sleeping pills. However, if other drugs are available through having been prescribed to another member of the family or a close acquaintance, they will be used. The increased use of barbiturate with age can be explained along similar lines. Insomnia is more frequent as age advances; barbiturates are prescribed more often and hence are more readily available. It has been suggested that elderly people resort to the use of coal-gas because they are often alone in the home for long periods and therefore less likely to be disturbed. In addition they may be influenced by the fact that they do not have young children whose lives would be endangered by the toxic fumes. It has also been suggested that they use gas because, in their younger days, it was considered to be one of the main methods of self-poisoning, and they have carried this tradition with them. Fortunately, the hazards of coal-gas have at last been realized and the authorities have reduced its carbon monoxide content and hence its toxicity. This may have affected the death rate. However, the increased use of pilot lights in gas appliances and the removal of its characteristic smell may provide a new hazard, particularly for the elderly. People may die or suffer severe brain damage through the effects of asphyxiation (sheer lack of oxygen) rather than through the more traditional carbon monoxide effect of coal-gas. The result is much the same, but the new hazard is less easy to detect and may in the long run cause more accidents, although perhaps fewer attempted and completed suicides.

Seasonal Variations

It has often been demonstrated that there are seasonal variations in completed suicide with peaks occurring in spring and autumn. In Edinburgh, for example, April and November have suicide figures which account for a quarter of the annual total. This reported seasonal distribution has brought forth all manner of "explanations", but none have been very convincing. It is known that there is a high risk of suicide among people who are clinically depressed and that special preventative care has to be taken. These depressive states do not always come to the notice of a psychiatrist. The lay reaction to such states is one of "you will be all right when winter is over" or "once you have had your holiday you will feel better". If the feeling of low spirits has not been alleviated by these events, then the despair may be the deeper because any hope which was aroused has been destroyed. However, this seeming seasonal variation has little practical value. So far as attempted suicide is concerned, the autumn peak is paralleled but the spring one is not. Even so, the peak is so slight that, unlike suicide, no two months account for any sizeable proportion of the total figure.

Of importance in manning a treatment centre or being available for calls for help is an awareness of the day-to-day variation in suicidal attempts. The peak time for attempts is at weekends, particularly Sunday, while fewest episodes occur in the middle of the week. Public holidays, too, tend to produce an upsurge in admissions. The importance of this finding is that peak periods for suicidal attempts occur at times when professional staffs and many lay advisory bodies are not available. Notable exceptions to this are agencies such as suicide prevention centres and the telephone Samaritans. The presence of the Samaritans as a helping agency is well known through-out the United Kingdom, while in the United States there is now a directory of suicide prevention centres which gives the location and the telephone numbers of all known centres. It is clear even from this limited information that people so distressed as to behave in a suicidal way require help and understanding *when they need it*, not just when the professional worker is available. It is still not easy for a distressed person to be received into hospitals for help until the act has been committed, yet hospitals are fre-quently the only establishments where staff work on a 24-hour basis. Unfortunately, emergency hospital staff seldom include members of a mental health team. While it is encouraging to note that round-the-clock services are becoming more and more available throughout the world, there is still a long way to go.

Marital Status

It has been suggested, albeit very tentatively, that there are associations between completed suicide and some aspects of marital status. Stengel and others have suggested that there is a relationship which exists between persons who live alone and suicide; this includes persons who are single, widowed, or divorced. Disrupted marriages which have not been legally terminated but which have reached the point of divorce are not usually commented upon because of the lack of reliable statistics. It is much more easy to be accurate about marital state when dealing with people whose suicidal behaviour has *not* resulted in death. Single women under the age of 35 years are more at risk than single men of the same age, but over that age the sex ratio is reversed. For married people women are more likely to attempt suicide. It is of interest that while married women tend to have higher rates than single women of comparable age, this is not true for men. For the under-35 age group both single and married men have comparable rates, but in the older age group the rate for single men is double that of their married counterparts. The rates for the widowed are low, while those for the divorced and separated are very high. At least for Edinburgh these findings have been remarkably constant over the years. The quality of marriage as an indication of interpersonal relationships is clearly important and will be discussed later.

Social Class

There are many attitudes and behaviours which are popularly considered to be typically upper class, middle class, or working class. Undoubtedly these classes differ in attitudes and behaviour, but to delineate these differences has proved to be incredibly difficult. The authors do not agree with those writers who use indices of social status, such as the Registrar-General's classification of occupation, as valid indicators of these class attitudes. The concept of social class too frequently carries with it ready-made preconceptions about attitudes and ways of life, and it is timely to remind the reader that the social class categories in common usage have been created as a convenient summary of economic activity and are not concerned in any way with the character of the people so classified. Nevertheless, most writers in this field have considered suicidal behaviour in relation to social class as thus defined.

As indicated on page 8, two groups of *suicides* have been identified in terms of age. A similar bimodality of distribution exists for social class. There is an association with affluence at one end of the scale and with poverty at the other. On the whole, however, as Sainsbury pointed out, persons who complete the suicidal act are most often found in the middle and upper social classes. For *attempted suicide* the picture is very different, and the Edinburgh studies have over the years shed much light on this. In this city approximately one-tenth of the annual admissions to hospital following a suicidal attempt come from the combined social classes I and II, one-tenth from social class III, one-fifth from class IV, and the remainder from class V.* It has been suggested that the financially well-to-do, following a suicidal attempt, obtain preferential care by being treated at home while the poor are sent to hospital. Although this is probably due more to the availability of adequate accommodation for home nursing rather than to money, it has been empirically investigated. Making the assumption that general practitioners are unlikely to take the risk of treating patients *found unconscious* at home, we have found that, both according to social class and area of domicile, *unconscious* hospitalized patients show the same picture as *all* hospitalized attempted-suicide patients. There is no doubt that in trying to understand the behaviour of these people, social class is largely irrelevant. We suggest that persons who have suicidal behaviour as a common experience are more like each other than they are like persons of their own social class who do not manifest this behaviour.

In addition to such secular factors as age, sex, and social class there are several areas of common experience in the history of people who behave suicidally. Some of these relate to early childhood and others to later periods in life. All these can be conveniently considered under three main headings. The first is concerned with the disruption of close interpersonal relationships, the second involves other emotional problems, while the third deals with problems in the wider social sphere.

Childhood Experiences

Many people in the world of psychology, psychiatry, and social work have been interested in the role played by early experience in the development of personality. Writers as varied in their outlook as Freud, Erikson, and the early behaviourists such as J. B. Watson have placed great store on early relationships within the family. Other writers, among whom Bowlby is the most noted, have concerned themselves with the effects of maternal

---

* The Registrar-General's social class groupings are intended to provide a convenient summary of economic activity. Class I comprises professional occupations; class II intermediate, middle management occupations; class III skilled occupations; class IV partly skilled occupations; and class V unskilled occupations. For further education students, social class in this sense is determined by father's occupation.

deprivation and the emotional problems of early childhood. There are also many works concerning the emotional development of children which are concerned with disturbances in parent–child relationships. These have been well reviewed by Casler and by Clarke and Clarke. The latter authors stress two main types of deprivation, one of which is socio-economic and cultural and therefore shows wide variations in time and place, while their second includes five distinct forms of deprivation. These are social isolation, cases of cruelty and neglect, institutional upbringing, adverse child-rearing practices, and separation experiences. Among the factors which they consider relevant in deprivation are the duration and intensity of the experience, previous experience of similar deprivation, the age of occurrence, and other aspects which can be thought of as being influenced by the personality of the child at the time. In summary they offer four main conclusions. Firstly, that there are considerable differences between children in vulnerability. Secondly, that individuals show varying degrees of recovery even from severe deprivation. Thirdly, gross deprivation such as prolonged isolation usually has profound psychological effects. Lastly, they comment on the remarkable ability of children to tolerate wide variations in their early experience.

In studies which we have conducted, we were able to demonstrate that there exists a relationship between suicidal behaviour and deviations in the normal child–parent relationship. Associations between suicidal behaviour and contact with the Royal Scottish Society for the Prevention of Cruelty to Children (RSPCC), truancy from school, being taken into care as a child, road accidents in childhood, and juvenile delinquency were established. Here we present two cases which, to some extent, demonstrate these associations.

CASE 1. *Mrs. H. P.*

This lady, fifth of a family of eight children, was first admitted to the Poisoning Treatment Centre at the age of 20. At the time of her admission both her parents were alive and living together. She had spent her entire childhood, until her marriage, with her natural parents. Prior to her admission to the Poisoning Treatment Centre an elder sister had been admitted on four occasions following acts of deliberate self-poisoning, the last one being fatal. As a child Mrs. H. P. frequently truanted and frequently had been kept off school to help with domestic chores—not always because her mother was ill. Interestingly, the patient's own children have truanted and have also had many absences because of her frequent domestic and social troubles. Both her parents have been at odds with the law, while she herself has had several appearances in court for "breach of the peace", and some years ago she was placed on probation for endangering the lives of her children while attempting to gas herself. As a result of this episode three of her four children were taken into care. Although Mrs. H. P. was never involved in a road accident as a child, one of her children, then aged 2 years, was knocked down and seriously injured while playing, unaccompanied, over a mile from home. Since her first admission to the Centre in 1962 Mrs. H. P. has been admitted on at least twenty-four other occasions, most of which were following suicidal acts. The other admissions were the result of her drinking. Although on some of her admissions this lady was clearly depressed, the underlying diagnosis is that of a psychopathic personality with habituation to alcohol and drugs.

CASE 2. *The White Family*

Figure 1 presents the pedigree of a family whom we shall call, for purposes of this study, the "White family". It demonstrates dramatically

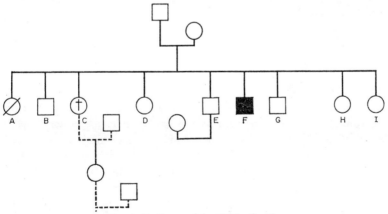

FIG. 1. Pedigree of the White family.

how a peculiar child–parent relationship pattern can be handed down from generation to generation in the particular context of suicidal behaviour. The first generation of this remarkable family showed no psychopathology on the female side until the grandmother of our series poisoned herself.

In grandfather's family, however, there was much alcoholism and mental illness. Indeed, one of his siblings has spent more than 60 years in mental hospital. This sister's admission to hospital followed involvement in a road accident in which her mother was killed. Great-grandfather remarried and none of the children of his first marriage enjoyed a good relationship with their step-mother. Grandfather, who had been treated frequently for alcoholic psychosis, was the first of three generations to reach the Poisoning Treatment Centre. The second generation consisted of nine children, one of whom, A, died in infancy. Only one of the remaining eight children, F, has not been admitted to the Centre. In addition, the spouses of two of the second generation have indulged in suicidal behaviour. The daughter of C was the first and, so far as is known, the only member of the third generation to be admitted. At the age of 16 years both she and her mother were cohabiting in the same house. She had had a row with her cohabitee, who had also passed through the Unit having been stabbed while in prison. In all, the twelve members of this family who have indulged in suicidal behaviour have, between them, done so on more than thirty-five occasions. Second generation C's last act was fatal.

In addition to these two cases there are many instances of parent–child admissions but perhaps none which demonstrate quite so clearly the severity of psycho-social pathology such as mental illness, alcoholism, neglect, cruelty, delinquency, and crime. In the main, these are people who grow up in an environment in which impulses tend to be acted out. Petty crime, prostitution, and many other forms of degradation have been witnessed as part of their daily lives. They have been reared in a climate where actions speak louder than words, where impulsiveness is dominant and where people live from day to day, having weak ties to the past and little investment in the future.

One of the most traumatic experiences for a child must be the breaking up of the nuclear home, and the relationship between this experience and subsequent attempted or completed suicide has been frequently demonstrated. It is suggested that there is a more basic trauma which involves the fracture of close, interpersonal contacts or events in a child's life which prevent the establishment of close, satisfying relationships. However, so much has been written about the effect of the broken home that it is felt that the reader should have the benefit of these research findings and theories as they relate to suicidal behaviour.

Broken Homes

Bowlby gathered together many of the psychoanalytic concepts and theories about the vital importance of early mother–child relationships in personality development exemplified by Fig. 1. Among persons who behave in a suicidal manner there is a large group who, at the time of their act, have been suffering from a depressive illness. While some studies have shown that such patients have suffered early parent loss to a greater extent than non-depressed individuals, this picture is by no means uniform. Munro, for instance, has shown that when all causes of separation are considered almost half of a group of "normals" suffered such parent loss. The Edinburgh studies have shown that among the persons who attempt to kill themselves or who succeed in doing so, there are large numbers who have some underlying abnormality of personality, and perhaps it is this factor which has been responsible for so many attempts to demonstrate a relationship between broken homes and attempted suicide. The varying orientations of the researchers involved has led them to consider many different aspects of parental loss and, unfortunately because of this, to employ different criteria in their studies, thus negating the possibility of true comparisons. Toolan's work perhaps typifies psychoanalytic thought as it relates to suicidal behaviour and depression. His theory is that the common denominator in all depressive reactions is the loss of the love object, and that when this occurs in "latency" (a period when sexual impulses are presumed to be smouldering but quiescent and occurring between the ages of 6 and 12 years of age) and late adolescence the child hates the love object, who, he feels, has betrayed and deserted him. Subsequently guilt feelings arise which ultimately result in self-punishment, of which suicidal behaviour is one form. At an empirical level Greer and Gunn have demonstrated that among a group of patients who have attempted suicide and who had suffered parental loss in childhood, a considerable number are sociopaths, and that this diagnosis is applied more than four times more often than in a group of attempters who come from homes which had remained intact. They also point to the fact that whereas almost one-half of the group from broken homes had attempted suicide following a recent disruption of a close interpersonal relationship, only in one-quarter of the "intact" home group was the attempt so preceded. These findings are very similar to those found in Edinburgh, and certainly confirm our opinion that parental loss may be a contributory factor to the inability of some persons to create and maintain satisfying relationships.

These early experiences are known to influence later behaviour, and it is not surprising that where there has been a disrupted start there is little to build on. Thus in maturity, as in childhood, ample evidence is found of poor interpersonal relationships.

Marital Disharmony and Love Problems

This is another area which, like broken homes, has been shown to have strong associations with persons who attempt or commit suicide. Again, because of the different orientations, interests, and methods used by researchers, it is difficult to assess the true extent of these problems as contributory factors, and it is not our intention here to do more than to point out that most studies have shown that actual or threatened disruption of close relationships due to conflict appears to be strongly associated with acts of attempted suicide. The importance of this association will be discussed later, but it should be borne in mind that, as pointed out in the section on broken homes, the inability to maintain satisfying relationships may result from aberrations of personality. This being so, one cannot and should not look for "cause and effect" where specific problems are concerned. This is not to say that a person could not attempt suicide because of the distress (or depression) caused by such an event but, as Robins has pointed out, amatory disturbance is greater in cases where there has also been a diagnosis of psychopathy or sociopathy.

In this section some of the implications in suicidal acts of traumatic events in the life of the attempter are discussed and it is pointed out that some of these social events may have had lasting effects on the development of personality. It is indicated, at least by implication, that such events may, if contiguous with a suicidal act, be seen as factors which precipitate the act. But if there is no close time relationship, experiences which have a profound effect on the development of personality may be indirectly causal of other precipitating factors which are concerned with the breakdown of inter-personal relationships. There are experiences other than those discussed so far which have such effects and whose presence can perhaps be best expressed in terms of their social implications.

Emotional Problems

Emotions such as jealousy, anger, spite, and hate can have serious social consequences when acted out, and cause crisis situations both in the lives of the person who experiences them and of the persons to whom they are directed. Many studies have shown clear evidence of a strong association between disrupted interpersonal relationships and suicidal behaviour and while the breach is, as pointed out, frequently described as a "precipitating" factor for suicidal behaviour, there is little doubt that these basic emotions may be more directly causal of the subsequent act. It is well-nigh impossible to demonstrate an absolute causal relationship between these emotions and suicidal behaviour, but many researchers have provided information of a quite convincing nature to show that, at least for children and adolescents, such emotions not infrequently result in attempted suicide. Teicher attempted to formulate a theory about this and suggested that a person indulging in non-fatal suicidal behaviour was so basically insecure that he could not direct his hate either completely inwards or act it out on the person at whom "the feeling" was directed. Jacobziner, in studies of attempted suicide in young people, believed that the high incidence of jealousy and anger he found was in many cases an act of rebellion against a restraining loved person. He postulated that the attempt was an effort to frighten the loved one into a change of attitude and behaviour. Faigel stated that this desire to punish others by attempting to kill themselves was one of the most frequent motives in acts of attempted suicide in young children. The inability of children to punish their parents directly may cause them to attempt their own destruction. Zilboorg, writing about suicide among primitive peoples, believed that spite was a frequent motivation and suggested that this was a typical and universal reaction.

Thus many researchers have agreed that children who nurse such high emotional feelings become overwhelmed with guilt and direct the aggression against themselves. The fantasy that parents will feel sorry thus incorporates the desire to punish. Although most of the comment on spite or anger has been concerned with the reactions of young people, there are many clear-cut instances of such behaviour to be found in studies of suicidal behaviour among adults. Jealousy has also been noted as a motive for suicidal behaviour, but whether one can reasonably divide this emotion from the emotions such as spite or hate which it provokes is extremely doubtful. It is of interest, however, that the Edinburgh studies have shown that among married women pathological jealousy in the husband was found in almost a quarter of the cases. Indeed, the persistent suspicions and questions of the "jealous husband" were frequently found to be a precipitating factor for the attempt. In all but a tiny proportion of such cases the husbands themselves reported that their jealousy had been completely unfounded.

Bereavement

Much of the research into the relationship between broken homes and suicidal behaviour incorporates references to bereavement and has been discussed briefly under that heading. In addition to the effects of the loss caused by bereavement on the development of personality, there is evidence that it may for some be an actual precipitating factor. The desire to identify with a dead person has been found by many researchers and appears to present in two distinct but overlapping ways. In the case of the elderly this desire is at its highest, and such classification can be readily accepted at its face value since the distress caused by the loss of a partner of very many years' standing can leave a gap which the elderly have no desire to bridge. Bereavement has also been shown to have a strong association with depressive illness, and this can be the underlying factor in suicidal behaviour.

Bereavement, however, need not be concerned with the loss of a partner or with the loss of a parent. It is sometimes forgotten that the loss of a child can also be involved, with all the consequences of distress and depression. In addition, where the bereavement has involved the loss of a child one can sometimes also detect *anniversary* associations. That is to say, suicidal behaviour can be repeated on the anniversary of either the death or the funeral of the lost child. It is likely, however, that the bereavement is not resurrected only at these times; it has never been truly resolved.

CASE 3. *Mr. and Mrs. Q.*

This couple's only daughter died when she was 6 years old and both parents reacted very badly to her loss. The husband began to invest more and more time in his business, which prospered under his excessive drive. Unfortunately, he sought no comfort at home and offered none to his wife but instead began drinking quite heavily. Meantime Mrs. Q. gave up working in her husband's business because she could not face the sympathy from workers, customers, and friends. She withdrew from practically all her usual activities, but apart from this she was not immobilized and was not in a clinically depressed state. She turned her energies into maintaining the home in an obsessional manner, and this included the maintaining of her lost daughter's room as though she were still alive. Dolls were on the bed and clothes kept clean and pressed ready for use. There were pictures of the child in every room and the mother did all the things by herself that she had done with the child—went her favourite walks, listened to children's gramophone records, etc. For the next 2 years the husband started drinking really heavily on the anniversary of daughter's death and the bout which lasted until the day of the anniversary of the funeral was enjoined by Mrs. Q. On both occasions it culminated in a suicide pact which resulted in both being admitted to the Poisoning Treatment Centre.

It is of interest that on both occasions the method adopted, coal-gas plus barbiturates, would, but for intervention, have caused death. There is equally little doubt that there was a very clear desire to join the dead child, but because of intoxication the planning went wrong.

Problems Involving the Wider Social Sphere

FINANCIAL PROBLEMS

Problems of finance have perhaps been more in the public eye in suicidal behaviour than many of the other associated factors. Presumably this has been due to the spate of suicides which followed the Wall Street crash and because of the many dramas which have sprung therefrom. Money, or the lack of it, can, of course, cause great stress for many, but the role that financial problems have really played in suicide and attempted suicide is far from clear.

There are two aspects of difficulties with money, one reflecting a chronic state of impoverishment and the other indicating a specific precipitating agent, if not of the suicide attempt, at least of the often-associated depressive illness. One of the difficulties in discussing this particular factor is due to the lack of unanimity in the definition of poverty, which varies with time and national circumstances. No doubt many of the people who have killed themselves following adverse business situations would have, in their earlier years, known poverty which, even though their business became insolvent, they would never again have to experience. Because of the difficulties of definition, there have been wide variations in the estimates of the involvement of financial difficulties either as a chronic state or as a precipitating factor from as little as 10 per cent to as high as 62 per cent. Of course, when asked *Why did you do it?* the attempter, who frequently has not truly formulated a reason, will turn to concrete things to provide the answer and, where the culture emphasizes the importance of affluence, there are few people who could claim that they had no financial problems. The fact that to a greater or lesser degree the normal person worries about his finances causes further difficulties, since when a person becomes depressed these worries are frequently grossly exaggerated and may be given as the *reason* for a suicidal attempt when in fact the attempt is but a symptom of the presenting illness.

EMPLOYMENT PROBLEMS

Among the employed, fears of redundancy or dismissal and fears of promotion are common sources of anxiety and distress. In today's fast-changing technological society these fears have generally become much more common and present an especial fear among people who have passed middle age. It has become common practice to select work personnel on an age basis for two main reasons. The first is that in a stable non-changing occupation more service can be anticipated, and the second is that where change can be anticipated the younger man or woman is more likely to be amenable to change and retraining. So much has this been emphasized that in the United States there is now legislation which seeks to remove the bias of preference for youth in the employment market when this is the only factor which discriminates. It is doubtful, however, if legislation can remove the fears, anxieties, and depressions, sometimes culminating in suicidal behaviour, which can and do arise in relation to work. So far as unemployment is concerned, there are two major classes of people involved: those who are temporarily out of work and are anxious to resume, and those to whom unemployment can be seen almost as a way of life. The latter situation is especially true of societies like that existing in Great Britain where social security schemes have reached a relatively advanced stage. Unfortunately, in some circumstances this advancement has created a situation where for some of the lower-paid occupations it can be financially more advantageous to be unemployed than to work gainfully. It has been more common in studies of suicidal behaviour to focus attention on unemployment as an associated factor. Estimates of the importance of employment problems or the problem of unemployment have varied greatly, and this has been largely due to the difficulty in assessing the importance of paid employment among women, especially married women who may or may not be dependent on a subsidiary income. The Edinburgh studies have undoubtedly shown that estimates of the work record of men who have attempted suicide show at least one-third of them to have experienced frequent or prolonged periods of unemployment which was unrelated to work capability or to its availability. The same studies showed that unemployment was stated to be a major precipitating factor for more than one-third of the males involved and was present as a contributing factor for the act for almost half of the men and a quarter of the women. It ranked fourth in the order of elicited precipitating factors and was exceeded only by the factors of financial difficulty, drink, and marital disharmony.

Just as some adults have worries about work performance or promotion, it has been suggested that among adolescents and children who are still at school or in further education, there have been difficulties with performance which could be seen as predisposing reasons for attempted suicide, and it may well be that these are equivalents.

CRIME

In persons who have abnormal personalities there is an increased frequency in the occurrence of both criminal and suicidal behaviour although these behaviours need not be causally related. The presence of crime in the background of a person who has indulged in a suicidal act is usually interpreted as being indicative of an aberration of personality, and in the majority of cases this may well be an accurate interpretation. It has to be argued, however, that before the diagnosis of personality disorder can be made there must be long-term indications of it or evidence of more recent physical or physiological changes (e.g. accident) which could bring about a radical change of personality. When considering the possible associations between suicidal behaviour and crime one must also take into consideration the subjective interpretation of crime and punishment. Frequently, fear of prosecution or imminent detection can be seen as an immediate precipitant for suicidal behaviour whether or not there has been a background of delinquent behaviour.

There has been a very wide variation in the estimates of crime as an associated or precipitating factor for suicidal behaviour, often due to the selection of deviant populations for study. In studies where there has been no conscious selection, crime has ranked fairly high both as a precipitant and as a factor present in the background of the attempter. In our own studies there was also a clear relationship between the presence of a criminal background and the primary diagnosis of "character disorder", and both were present in approximately one-third of the population studied.

LONELINESS

In his London study, Sainsbury showed a significant relationship between suicide and loneliness which has also been widely reported as a motive for all suicidal behaviour whether fatal or not, and this relationship appears to hold good amongst older people. Batchelor and Napier found that more than half of a group of persons aged between 40 and 60 years gave loneliness as the precipitating factor for attempting suicide. Evidence has also been provided by Stengel that the rate for isolation as a precipitating factor for attempted suicide may be almost four times the rate for isolation among the general population. It is possible to regard the relationship between suicidal behaviour and loneliness in two distinct ways. There are many people who become lonely and would rather have company, the absence of which is of such concern that a process develops which culminates in a suicidal attempt. There is another group, however, who, because of psychological illness or socio-economic failure, desire privacy. Among this latter group this privacy may even be sought in a context of social anonymity, and Clausen and Kohn found that men in rooming houses tended to drift there for these reasons. It has also been found that there is a tendency for suicide to accompany this downward drift because men who have experienced this drop in social status see it as a way out of their predicament. Schneider suggested that nearly all of the theories about the relationship of sociological factors and mental illness could be subsumed under eight categories, one of which was social isolation. Such isolation can reflect character abnormality and can precipitate mental illness and hence suicidal behaviour. But in situations where it is not sought, isolation can be so socially distressing that suicidal acts are precipitated. It has been suggested that of all the psychodynamic factors associated with suicidal behaviour, isolation may be the one which most clearly distinguishes those whose intent is the most lethal.

Leese, investigating school-age suicides, found that chronic social isolation was the most striking feature, while Jan-Tausch suggested that the critical difference between children who "failed" in their attempts and those who "succeeded" was that the former had a close relationship with someone. He suggested that in suicide the individual had either withdrawn to the point where he could no longer identify with any person or idea or could not establish close supportive relationships. This withdrawal can of course be symptomatic of the most commonly associated illness—depression—while the inability to make and maintain close supportive relationships is quite consonant with the younger group of suicides which were identified in studies conducted in Edinburgh.

There have been many psychodynamic theories offered to explain the relationship between isolation and suicidal behaviour. Stengel postulated that the lack of a secure parent–child relationship could have lasting consequences for a person's ability to make and maintain firm relationships in later life. In their studies of adolescent suicide, Jacobs and Teicher suggested that the subjects usually had numerous and serious problems which progressively isolated them from experiencing normal interpersonal relationships. They cite the long periods of extreme parental conflict which frequently lead to complete alienation. A subsequent suicidal attempt, they say, may result from a failed romance which probably began as an effort to re-establish a meaningful relationship. It has been suggested that where peer group relations were good this could compensate greatly for even a severely disorganized family life. These findings are generally substantiated by the findings of researchers in this field that suicide is much less frequent among married persons except in the case of the younger married population. It is extremely likely that this situation arises from the fact that, in an effort to re-establish close interpersonal relationships, marriages may be entered into for reasons which are almost calculated to destroy it. Schrut suggested that adolescent females, estranged from their parents, frequently relied on a boyfriend to become the "substitute parental image". Our studies have certainly shown that the demands made by adolescent girls on their boy-friends prior to a suicidal attempt were of a very testing nature, and the case cited on page 38 was fairly typical of many which have passed through the Poisoning Treatment Centre.

It is now well known that people who talk about attempting to kill themselves frequently do so, *and that all such threats should be taken with great seriousness*. It follows, however, that where there is actual social isolation or feelings of it, this call for help is both difficult to make and to receive. As postulated earlier, the intent of suicidal behaviour may not be death but to call attention to feelings of helplessness, and we have tried to show that if the cry is not heard, what may have started as an effort to create relation-ships or to restore them may end in death. It is imperative, therefore, that for the socially isolated many lines of easily attainable communication be created and equally, when a call for help is made, the listener *should be sympathetic* so that another fracture in relationships does not result.

ALCOHOL

It is widely known that alcoholism or heavy drinking is associated with suicidal behaviour. Indeed, alcoholism has been described as "chronic suicide". Estimated numbers of alcoholics found among suicides vary from 15 to 50 per cent, while estimates of its association with attempted suicide are equally alarming, especially among men. Many alcoholics and bout drinkers are anxious or inadequate people who drink for relief. They are often persons with severe character disorders who are "crisis prone", and having precipitated such crises they attempt to escape by the use of drink, seeking oblivion. According to psychoanalytic theory the alcohol addict has an oral narcissistic personality. That is to say he has been frustrated at the oral stage of development and has become disappointed by his mother. Without going fully into the analytic theories of latent homosexuality, suffice it to say that, once again, a background which highlights difficulties with interpersonal relationships can be seen. Alcohol, because of its sedative and hypnotic effects, helps to relieve mental tension and depression but does nothing to cure them, and there develops a need to "increase" intake to ensure continued relief. This in turn brings about surreptitious drinking, guilt feelings about drink, and eventually loss of control over it. It does nothing to create the kind of relationships which are sought. Tolerance diminishes and drinking becomes obsessive until finally *all* defences fail. During this process there are further estrangements from key people until there is little to live for. The usual medical and social reaction to heavy drinking is to point out the dangers of physical, mental, or social ruin, and this often aggravates the situation to such an extent that a "don't-care-if-I-die" attitude develops. When this situation arrives, life has no real meaning and defences are diminished. Suicidal behaviour is then an easy step to take—perhaps even a welcome one. It must be remembered that alcohol can reduce inhibitions and so increase impulsive behaviour so that "escape" reactions to stressful situations are facilitated. It is not unknown for an attempter to be unable to carry out his wishes until he has some "Dutch courage", and cases are frequently reported where patients said that they wanted to die but could not face up to the act without first getting drunk. Our studies have shown that almost 40 per cent of men and 7 per cent of women had alcoholism as a primary or secondary diagnosis, while half of the men and a quarter of the women were either drunk or had taken drink at the time of their suicidal attempt. These are fairly typical of the findings from researches carried out in Europe and the United States.

DRUGS

The dependence on drugs to relieve tensions and facilitate social relationships produces much the same picture as for alcoholism, and it is known that one of the characteristics of the addict is his inability to maintain social relationships. He is frequently described as a "loner" who, when in the company of fellow addicts, tends to live alongside them rather than with them. Corrected for age, the suicide rate for persons addicted to main-line drugs is about fifty times higher than for non-addicts.

Studies in Edinburgh have shown that people who are dependent on soft drugs as a group are more likely to become "repeaters". Of an original cohort of 511 persons who had attempted suicide there were 26 who were dependent on drugs. During the 2 years following discharge from the Poisoning Treatment Centre almost half of them had been re-admitted following further episodes. In the same period, 8 of the cohort had killed themselves and of the 8, 4 were alcoholics, 1 was alcoholic and drug dependent, and 2 were drug dependent.

Drug-taking is unfortunately very much on the increase throughout the world, and the addicts are becoming younger and younger until there are many children of 12 years and under who are addicted to main-line and other drugs. Experimentation with the psychedelic drugs has brought about further suicide hazards as subjects have acted in response to hallucinations and delusions. It has been reported that persons have thrown themselves to death in the belief that they could fly, or to act on the hallucination that cars on roads were toys which could be picked up.

It has also been suggested that where there have been suicidal thoughts before taking LSD, these wishes have been intensified. Seiden has argued that this condition can lead to suicide attempts while under LSD or attempts which come after the "trip". He suggests that there can be an intrusion of suicidal ideas resulting from a panic state in an individual who has had no previous suicidal thoughts when he believes that a "bad trip" will never end. Seiden also cites cases of LSD-induced fantasy suicides where the subject believes that death is necessary for altruistic reasons and that he "must die to save the world". Cases are also reported where the drug magnifies or distorts psychopathology or depression. Panic becomes intensified by the blurring of the events which brought on the episode and whether or not it can be ended. Attempted suicide in this state may resemble the motivation to escape from psychic pain that occurs in other drugged states. An understanding of the association between drugs and suicidal behaviour is still far from clear, but there is sufficient evidence to be quite categorical in stating that experimentation with drugs is extremely dangerous.

This chapter discussed some of the social events which appear to be associated with suicidal behaviour. Sometimes the factors involved at the time of the suicidal act are the result of underlying physical illness or disability, mental illness, mental subnormality, or personality abnormality. The social factors described are frequently multiple and are often stresses of long standing. The presence of interacting social factors frequently tells us more about the patient's personality than about the motivation for the act itself, and this will be discussed in Chapter 2. Our studies have shown that there are significant relationships between the social factors associated with suicidal behaviour and other forms of deviant behaviour which also appear to have their roots in aberrations of personality, and later the psychological characteristics of persons who behave suicidally will be discussed. It is dangerous to accept that there is a *causal* relationship between these social and other factors frequently referred to as "precipitants" and suicidal behaviour. As already pointed out, although patients may be prepared to say "I did it because . . .", the interpretation of the motive and the intent may still have to be inferred since the role played by these social factors is still lacking clarity of definition.

CHAPTER 2

Psychiatric Findings

WE HAVE already commented on the difficulties in making international comparisons of suicide rates, and, of course, these difficulties extend to the field of psychiatric investigation and treatment. Because there is an international classification of psychiatric disorder, and because of the worldwide concern with the problem of suicidal behaviour, an attempt is made to tabulate some of the more pertinent findings for the guidance of the student. This chapter will be concerned with areas of study which are of interest to psychiatrists. These areas—psychiatric diagnosis; motive, premeditation, and intent; endangerment to life; method; treatment and disposal—are not exclusively the province of psychiatrists and will appear again in later chapters.

Psychiatric Diagnosis

The amount of psychiatric pathology found in attempted suicide varies considerably, depending on the clinician and on the place where the patient has been seen. In Edinburgh, for instance, Kessel and others have found that rather more than one-third of admissions to the Poisoning Treatment Centre are found to have no psychiatric illness at all; other investigations have found psychiatric illness, including personality disorder, in all their cases. The justifications of this latter finding are generally twofold: patients are deemed to have had a catharsis, the violence of the act discharging the tension which led up to it, so that without any other evidence the patient *must* have been ill at the time; the second reason is much more sweeping: since the person made an attempt he must *ipso facto* be psychiatrically sick. An aspect which has tended to confuse the issue of psychiatric illness has been the fact that many studies have been carried out on mental hospital

30

populations, ignoring the fact that less than half of those making a suicidal attempt are subsequently admitted to a psychiatric hospital. Many of these studies have shown a striking indifference to the need to delineate the characteristics of the populations from which their suicidal patients were drawn. A further complicating factor has been that the person who has behaved suicidally presents, in the first instance, with a physical problem, and for many reasons—not the least being staffing difficulties—persons unskilled in psychiatry tend to equate the severity of the physical state with the severity of the underlying problem. There is no such easy equation, and those who have used severity of physical damage to predict future mental state and further suicidal behaviour have failed. It follows that when the net is cast as wide as it is in Edinburgh, where all persons are screened no matter how limited the physical damage, the amount of observed psychiatric illness in a suicidal population drops. Studies where the net has not been cast wide must remain of dubious value in understanding the range of important factors involved. We firmly endorse Kessel's statement that *"distress drives people to self-poisoning acts, and distress is not the exclusive province of the mentally ill"*.

Kessel reasoned that a psychiatric diagnosis could only be made by the presence of *positive* features detected either from the history or on clinical examination. If all the information on the patient's mental state at the time of his act, obtained both from him and an informant, did not indicate any departure from his usual state, and if clinical examination after physical recovery failed to record any significant disorder, then there were no grounds for claiming that the patient was or had been psychiatrically ill. These are some of the criteria used in Edinburgh to delineate "formal psychiatric illness". A good cross-section of studies which present estimates of psychopathology in suicidal behaviour is presented in Table 1.

Table 1 is reproduced from the WHO paper on *Prevention of Suicide* and bears out our comments on the utility, or futility, of comparing psychiatric diagnoses across centres and cultures. A perusal of the table shows that where patients have been admitted to a general medical department rather than to one which is essentially psychiatric, there is closer agreement on the level of psychopathology than is the case when patients have gone to a psychiatric unit. Table 1 also demonstrates well the very wide variations in diagnoses. For instance, the presence of psychotic illness varies from 7 to 25 per cent while the presence of personality disorder ranges from 15 to

TABLE 1. MENTAL DISORDERS AMONG PERSONS WHO ATTEMPT SUICIDE

Reference and place of study	Type of population	Size of sample	% with mental disorders	Comments
Achté and Ginman 1966 (Helsinki, Finland)	Poison-control ward, consecutive admissions	100	97	14% psychoses 24% neuroses
Blanc et al., 1966 (Gironde, France)	Psychiat. dept. gen. hosp. admissions, 1960–4	500	100	25% functional and organic psychoses
Dahlgren, 1945 (Malmö, Sweden)	Gen. hosp. admissions, 1933–42	251	77	
Ettlinger and Flordh, 1955 (Stockholm, Sweden)	Referrals to psychiat. dept. gen. hosp.	500	94·8	16·6% psychoses
ames et al., 1963 (Western Australia)	Emergency ward admissions	100	80	22% psychotic disturbance at time of attempt
Kapamadžija, 1966 (Novi Sad, Yugoslavia)	Psychiat. centre admissions, 1952–66	180	100	7% psychoses (nondepressive) 11% neuroses
Kessel, 1965 (Edinburgh, Scotland)	Poison-control ward, consecutive admissions, 1962–3	165 male 350 fem.	74 80	32% ⎰ personality 16% ⎱ disorder only
Krupinski et al., 1965 (Victoria, Australia)	Under care of ment. health department	204 male 154 fem.	90·2 75·4	27·9% psychoses 20·2% psychoses
Prokůpek, 1967 (Czechoslovakia)	Psychiatrically examined of total 18,930 registered attempts, 1963–6	15,641	91 male 86 fem.	14% male ⎱ psychoses 12% fem. ⎰ 35% male ⎱ neuroses 52% fem. ⎰ 28% male ⎰ "psycho- 19% fem. ⎱ pathies"
Schmidt et al., 1954 (St Louis, USA)	Gen. hosp. admissions, 1952–3	109	100	15% psychopathic personality
Stengel & Cook, 1958 (London, England)		627	100	Each patient given a psychiatric diagnosis

32

32 per cent, being a common feature of all groups of attempted suicide whether seen in a casualty department or in a psychiatric unit.

Personality disorder is one of the least satisfactory of all psychiatric diagnoses. From the clinical standpoint its boundaries are vague, its signs and symptoms uncertain. Given these vague boundaries it is not surprising that this diagnostic category has become something of a waste-basket. As already suggested, some clinicians appear to have worked on the assumption that to attempt suicide is an abnormal act which must denote some mental disturbance. For a professional worker to work on the assumption that persons so driven as to attempt to do away with themselves are *mad* or *bad* is an impertinence. For it is shown in Edinburgh, for instance, that many wives of pathologically jealous husbands can, without being abnormal in any way, be so despairing as to make a suicidal attempt. Things which are put in waste-baskets are worthless, and when this refers to people prognosis must also of necessity be bad. In the helping professions of social work and medicine, the *fostering of hope* is a crucial aspect of treatment. This is particularly important when dealing with this group of patients who have already indicated by their behaviour that hope is a commodity in which they are sorely lacking.

A common form of personality disorder seen by mental health workers is one where drinking to excess or outright alcoholism is salient. In an early study carried out on attempted suicides under remand at Brixton Prison in 1913, East found that in 39 per cent of his 1000 cases alcoholism was wholly or partly the cause of the attempt. Considering the vintage nature of this study it was remarkably well designed, but the inferences which East drew from his findings epitomize our contentions regarding the importance of the parent population studied. While his data on his subjects was comprehensive, he compared his highly selected group with studies of completed suicide. By the nature of the location of his study, all females were excluded, as were presumably persons suffering from severe mental illness (hence his low rate of 3 per cent seen to be suffering from mental disorder). It is hardly surprising therefore that in attempting to differentiate his group of attempted suicides from a completed suicide group he concluded that mental illness caused more suicide while alcoholism caused more attempted suicide. Had he looked more carefully at the constricted nature of his cohort his inferences might have been somewhat different. The fallaciousness of his conclusions are high-lighted even further by the later work of Kessel and Grossman, who, in a study of persons who had been admitted to hospital suffering from alcoholism, found a completed suicide rate which was 75–80 times the expected rate for males of the same age in London. Despite these flaws, East's paper describes a population which is recognizably similar to that seen in Edinburgh's Poisoning Treatment Centre. Although a male prison population, it was also a remanded attempted suicide population, and appears to have been much more varied in its composition than many later studies in which the mentally ill were over-represented. It is interesting to find that Wassermyer, an investigator of the same era, corroborated East's findings on alcoholism but completely opposed his findings on the incidence of mental illness in attempted suicide. This contrary finding is not surprising since he collected his information from a psychiatric clinic.

Motive, Premeditation, and Intent

The varieties of situations which provoke people to behave in a suicidal fashion are innumerable. Although undoubtedly there is uniqueness in the way in which unhappiness can affect individuals, some degree of generalization is possible. In dealing with a patient who has poisoned or injured himself the student must try to view the immediate antecedents of the event in the context of the patient's usual way of life. To ask "Why did you do it?" is to pose a deceptively simple question. A person who claims that debt was the cause of his attempt may have been in a more or less permanent state of debt for years without ever having attempted suicide. The life situations of people who behave in this way are usually so disorganized that it is inevitable that there is a build-up of stress, and when the bubble bursts, any one of a host of so-called reasons acceptable to the patient, and perhaps too often to the clinician also, spring to mind. If such a reason is seen to exist in the patient's life history, then it is verified and becomes established as fact, as is demonstrated by the following case.

CASE 4

A 53-year-old patient admitted to the Poisoning Treatment Centre having cut both wrists was found to be depressed. On examination he said that he attempted to kill himself because there had been a discrepancy in the funds of a club of which he was chairman and that this had caused him to brood on his own deficiencies. The fact that at the time of the attempt he had been drinking heavily was played down by his family. The fact that the club treasurer had repaid the money and resigned, they felt, meant that there was now nothing to worry about.

Hospitalization for him was strongly opposed by his relations because the "reason" for his attempted suicide no longer existed. The patient was, however, persuaded to have treatment for his depression, but before it could be completed, while on pass from hospital he had a heavy bout of drinking, threw himself in front of a train, and was killed.

Some people react to stress in a limited number of easily recognized ways, physical withdrawal from stressful situations being common. In others there is no characteristic mode of response. Even when the patient's own account of things is taken in conjunction with the evidence of some key person, or with the considered opinion of the clinical team, it is usually found that motives are complex, contradictory, or even absent. Suffice it to say that motive is extremely difficult to assess with any degree of accuracy. Premeditation and intent are similarly thorny problems. Once again the patient, the key person, and the clinical team may come to different conclusions about the same overt behaviour.

We could well have included impulsiveness in the heading to this section, but believe that it would be misleading to view impulsiveness as a recognizable entity in this very complex pattern of behaviour. One aspect of impulsiveness is its role as a character trait, that is to say a relatively enduring feature of a person's behaviour. Another aspect is its use as a label for unplanned suicidal behaviour in cases where neither the patient, key witness, nor clinical team can elicit any evidence of careful planning in the act. Kessel's emphasis on the need to elicit positive signs and symptoms before labelling in the diagnostic sense is equally applicable when considering premeditation and impulsiveness. His astonishing finding that two-thirds of all acts of attempted suicide were impulsive is of the utmost importance: He said: "Five minutes, sometimes only one minute, before the act took place, the idea of taking poison was not in the person's mind. He may have, he often had, thought about doing it in the past. Hours of rumination may have preceded the determination which was formed in a single moment. But in the event, at the event, a feeling of despair arose, often suddenly, from a trivial cause, and was as suddenly acted upon."

CASE 5

A case which typifies Kessel's formulation is one of a 64-year-old lady who from humble beginnings had reared a family who were successful. Her mother, a very old lady, was taken to hospital 150 miles away, and although the effect of this was not immediately apparent to any member of the family, hindsight shows that either because of, or coincidental with, her mother's illness she began to ruminate about her uselessness and felt that the family no longer needed her, this despite the fact that her daughter called to see her nearly every day.

Her daughter had a business appointment in a large town distant from home but nearer to where the grandmother was hospitalized. The patient did not ask her daughter to take her with her, and to make the lengthy detour necessary to visit the hospital. When the daughter did not invite her to make such a trip this was taken by the patient to mean that indeed her family did not care for her any more.

A typical aspect of her depression had been that she found it hard to sleep and had been prescribed sleeping tablets. On returning that night feeling very sorry for herself she went to take her drugs, found herself faced with 60 sleeping tablets and, on the spur of the moment, took the lot. On examination she denied any notions of suicide until the instant before she took the drugs.

Much of what Kessel subsumes under impulsiveness can be attributed to its character trait aspects, but in other ways this term clearly refers to some decision-making process. We conceive of a dimension of decision making marked at one end by carefully planned acts which take into account all possible reactions from the environment; such acts may encompass the classical suicide of the depressive, the so-called rational suicide, and even the suicidal gesture, where the reactions expected from the environment are certainly taken into account, whether at a conscious level or not. At the other end of this dimension there is no planning, no assessment of reaction from the environment, and no immediate meaning to the act—*it just happens*. This group may include those described by Kessel as impulsive and those described as gamblers by Stengel and others.

As the quotation from Kessel shows, there is a ruminative as well as a decision-making aspect to suicidal acts. Our second dimension is therefore one ranging from complete absence to very obvious presence of premeditation. In other words, a person may dwell on the possibility of taking his own life and either act on it immediately or continue to ruminate on it. It may take some other stimulus to turn thought into a train of action. This stimulus is often the sight of a lot of pills at pill-taking time or a sudden quarrel. Semantically it is likely that *planning* and *premeditation* have been confused, and some case evidence to demonstrate their separate nature follows.

CASE 6. *Dr. A.*

The case of Dr. A. who, in a seriously depressed state, decided to end his life. He was in the habit of going on long walks over moorland by himself and decided that to leave the house to go on such a walk would not be questioned since he customarily was absent for many hours at a stretch. He knew from his knowledge of the terrain that he was likely to meet no one. On the day that he decided to kill himself, he left the house as usual taking with him a large quantity of sleeping pills. In the most desolate part of his route, which was reached not long after leaving home, he took his massive overdose.

Clearly this is a case showing premeditation and a high degree of planning which took into account all reasonable reactions from the environment. Not only was a large quantity of pills acquired discreetly but he knew that his long absence would cause no suspicion until it was too late. Under all foreseeable circumstances this behaviour and planning would have culminated in *suicide*. But a stray sheep led a shepherd and his dog to the spot too soon for death to occur. This fact, prompt action by the shepherd, and good resuscitation caused this act to become *attempted suicide*.

CASE 7. *Mrs. B.*

The case of Mrs. B., a fisherman's wife who was drinking in a quayside tavern having had a quarrel with her husband. While drinking, she became obsessed with the idea that the other drinkers were talking ill of her. With this false realization she rushed from the bar, ran across the road and leapt into the harbour, giving no thought to the consequences. In the event she was quickly rescued and suffered no great harm.

She was considered to have *attempted suicide*. However, because of her lack of planning it is possible to think of many consequences, all or any of which could have killed her, in which case she would have been classed as *suicide*.

CASE 8. Miss C.

Having had a tiff with her boyfriend, Miss C. made her way to a telephone box immediately outside the hospital which houses the ward which deals with self-poisoning and self-injury, knowing such a ward to exist. The time she chose was important, since it encompassed hospital visiting time when many people would be near by. She telephoned her boyfriend who lived in the vicinity and told him that if he did not come to see her immediately she would slash her wrists. The boyfriend did not arrive and to the horror of the passers-by she was seen to carry out her threat. Admission to the hospital was immediate, after which the boyfriend appeared and the tiff was resolved.

This could be classified as a *suicidal gesture* or as *parasuicide*. However, factors such as an infected razor blade, a deeper cut, or no immediate response on the part of the passers-by could have led to death.

These three cases present six possible logical outcomes, and illustrate the part played by chance in interacting with premeditation and planning. If we consider only the end results of these cases it is possible for the clinician or theorist to indulge in interpretations of the "Russian roulette" variety. That is to say, people leave the decision to live or to die in the hands of the gods, inviting chance to play a part. But it must be the case that chance by its very nature is quite independent of human actions. Chance itself is indeterminate, as can be seen from the three case histories, and so it is illogical to assume that people indulging in suicidal behaviour allow for it. Perhaps the reasoning behind the "Russian roulette" interpretation is that some people do not appear to care whether they live or die. Surely this is really to say that they are not motivated to live? Thus motivated a person may premeditate suicide but plan it imperfectly so as to lead to the faulty execution of the act. This action aspect of suicidal behaviour, along with premeditation and all those environmental and personal factors peculiar to each individual, determines the outcome of the act. Chance is simply a misleading term used to cover the host of individual factors applicable to any one individual but difficult to apply to groups of people. These three spheres of influence are shown in Fig. 2, and it can be seen that when the

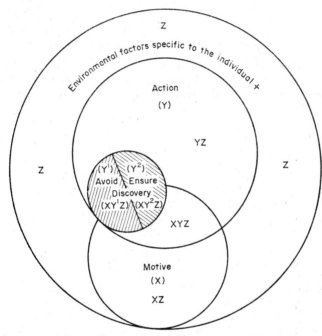

FIG. 2. The category indicated by (+) includes drug availability and toxicity (including individual pharmacological knowledge and tolerance) and any other potentially lethal method. It includes also chance factors involving the human actions of others which could not be foreseen by the attempter. This is essentially the area which leads to a decision about intent by an observer.

factors occur in different combinations different outcomes can be predicted. The varieties of outcome are exemplified by the case studies.

From the figure it can be seen that where premeditation X occurs in an individual's universe Z and action aimed at avoiding discovery Y^1 is at a maximum, risk of death is at its greatest. Death is least likely where factors X and Z are present in the absence of Y: a person may think about suicide and have access to a lethal method but takes no action to implement his thoughts. The reader can examine for himself other combinations of the three dimensions and can think of examples from his own experience. This examination might provide new insights into old cases.

It is believed that, without indulging overmuch in semantics, this model can accommodate all those forms of fatal and non-fatal suicidal behaviour labelled variously as attempted suicide, parasuicide, pseudocide, gestures, as well as suicide, accidental suicide, and failed suicide. Each and every one of these terms has attempted to accommodate some real aspects of suicidal behaviour, but all too often this has been done to the detriment of some other aspect of the same behaviour.

Endangerment to Life

In studies of suicidal behaviour there has been a tendency to look at life endangerment in two ways: to try to assess how lethal the patient thought his attempt was, or to attempt to evaluate the toxicological results and the expertise of nursing and medical staff, thus arriving at a seemingly more objective assessment. It is shown in our case histories that *true* endangerment to life must depend on a host of factors; the general properties of the drug when taken in excess, side effects of the drug if taken in excess, the interaction of the drug with other drugs or alcohol, individual differences in reaction to a given drug, the level of habituation of the patient to a drug, the time lag between ingestion of the drug and being taken to hospital, the skill of medical and toxicological staff in initiating appropriate treatment, and so forth. It is not possible to assess these factors with any degree of accuracy—they interact too much one with the other. In any case, it is more important to try to assess the patient's subjective notions of the danger involved and his level of sophistication about the method used, and to relate these to his degree of premeditation and planning.

The effectiveness of this approach can be seen by looking once again at the last three case histories. Had Dr. A. been Mr. A. and unversed in toxicology, he might have taken with him on his walk a bottle marked "poison", believing that to take a potion so labelled would ensure his death. It is well known that many substances are labelled "poison" according to the law but which in fact would not be lethal. For example, a solution of *X* fluid ounces of arsenic may kill, whereas the same quantity of some other solution intended for external use may be relatively harmless. This important change in the *Z* factor precludes death and ensures that Mr. A. becomes an attempted suicide.

In the case of Mrs. B., sheer impulsiveness could have resulted in her being run down and killed by a passing car. This would have resulted in her *accidental* death.

If Miss C., instead of threatening to cut herself, had threatened to ingest some poison, without being aware of its lethality, then she would have increased her chances of dying. Her act would have been less evident to passers-by and the effects, even although she had been able to proceed to hospital by herself, might have been too drastic to permit her survival. This outcome could now be classed as *suicide*.

Clearly changes in the environmental and personal universe *Z* are of vital importance in determining outcome, as is further demonstrated by the following case.

CASE 9. *Master D.*

A 13-year-old lad returns home warm and breathless after a game of football. He goes to the cupboard where the lemonade is kept, takes out a bottle labelled "lemonade" and gulps down a sizeable quantity of what in fact is weed-killer.

This case shows that there has been no suicidal premeditation or action and we can feel more happy with the obvious decision of *accidental poisoning*. It would be easy to suggest a slightly modified version of the same case where a suicidal attempt could at first glance be passed off as accidental.

To sum up, it is clear that endangerment to life, if such a concept is to be used at all, is most profitably assessed by looking at the patient's level of sophistication regarding the properties and effects of the method used. It is demonstrated also how this sophistication interacts with our planning dimension, which is clearly the *action* element of our model. Those whose planning is aimed at ensuring to live and who are unsophisticated both in their chosen method and in their knowledge of human behaviour, are perhaps the only group in the whole suicidal spectrum whose behaviour could be described as *gambling*. Even then, being unaware, they are not gambling in the sense in which it has been used by many authors.

Methods Used

People use methods which are available so that differences in the mode of suicide or attempted suicide are due to cultural, occupational, generational, and other factors not necessarily related to the suicidal behaviour in any meaningful way. Where firearms are readily available these will be used; where drugs are at hand, then these will be used. The butcher may use one of his own sharp knives; the housewife may place her head in the gas oven; the railway footplateman may leap in front of an express train. Seen in this way the method used in suicide or attempted suicide does not help in the understanding of such behaviour. Over the years the drugs used in self-poisoning have changed; crude chemical preparations are less often used, their place having been taken by preparations intended for therapeutic use. Kessel has pointed to the difference between these earlier preparations, which were recognized by one and all to be harmful, and modern preparations which are in the first instance therapeutic drugs. Poisons and drugs are no longer dissimilar; both the professional and the lay public are well aware that drugs given therapeutically can have undesired, adverse effects. Kessel contended, and the authors agree, that the lay public are much more knowledgeable about such drugs than is often assumed. People know now that they can take "poison" and live. Pharmacological advances and prescribing practices have made available a host of readily available preparations which, by and large, are much safer in overdose than were old-fashioned poisons which were ingested only with self-destructive intent. In the first instance the prescribing of drugs is a medical matter, but inevitably it has become a matter for grave public concern.

Treatment and Disposal

For those who die by their own hand we can offer no treatment, only a resolve to reduce the occurrence of such behaviour. Those whose suicidal behaviour does not have fatal consequences may or may not receive psychiatric treatment; indeed, many will not even be seen by a psychiatrist.

The illogicality of allowing a very junior doctor in an accident and emergency department to decide whether a patient warrants psychiatric assessment or not has been hammered home by researchers such as Kessel. Many studies which have been carried out on "attempted suicide" have studied patients who had been admitted to some psychiatric institution following their attempt. In such cases disposal has already taken place, and any findings put forward must be viewed with caution.

In a setting where all cases of suicidal behaviour admitted to a general hospital are seen by a psychiatrist, what is the pattern of disposal and treatment? About one-quarter of all patients seen in the Poisoning Treatment Centre in Edinburgh are sent to a psychiatric hospital for in-patient treatment. Of the remainder, half are given out-patient appointments while half receive no further psychiatric treatment. Availability of psychiatric beds and man-power are clearly important factors in determining who shall be treated and where. In this group of people there are many whose treatment lies in the hands of the social worker rather than in those of the psychiatrist, but again the availability of staff imposes limits on the nature and extent of social intervention.

Throughout this chapter making reference to specific diagnoses which may be associated with suicidal behaviour has been avoided. Our concern is with the social and psychological aspects of this behaviour since we believe that it is through the study of these aspects, rather than through processes of medical classification, that a better understanding of the phenomena of suicide will be reached. Of course there are psychiatric illnesses which are closely related to suicide. By far the most common of these is depression; and it has been found that the acts of patients who can be classified as having a psychiatric illness other than personality disorder tend to be more life-endangering than the acts of patients suffering from personality disorder or who have no demonstrable psychiatric illness. This is not to say, however, that the latter warrant less attention. All suicidal acts have serious connotations.

CHAPTER 3

Psychological Findings

An Overview of the Psychological Literature

The literature on the psychological assessment of suicidal behaviour is overwhelmingly American. All the major tests in the psychological armamentarium have been used, with varying degrees of sophistication, in the quest for the "suicidal personality". Clinically there is no such thing as an "attempted suicide personality" although, as pointed out, impulsive behaviour, poor interpersonal relationships, and undesirable social conditions are factors common to suicidal behaviour. It is not surprising that this psychological quest has been unsuccessful since results from projective techniques and questionnaire methods alike are equivocal in many instances and contradictory in others.

Two points about these studies should be made. Firstly, it is doubtful whether men who are in-patients in veterans' administration psychiatric hospitals and who at some time have threatened or attempted suicide, or who on some subsequent occasion commit suicide, are representative of the threatened suicide, attempted suicide, or committed suicide populations of the United States. Nonetheless, such men form the majority of persons tested; indeed, like a stage army, the test data of some of these individuals have appeared in different papers written at different times by different authors. The second point is that most American workers have a "continuum" view of suicidal behaviour, so that while persons who threaten, attempt, or commit suicide are sometimes considered as separate subgroups, their personality characteristics and dynamics are assumed to have common "suicidal" elements. All too frequently theoretical formulations about suicide are applied without modification to groups of persons who have threatened or attempted suicide, a procedure which facilitates confused thinking and inconclusive results. Even the workers in the Los Angeles

Suicide Prevention Center who have made such a valuable contribution to the understanding of suicidal behaviour do not appear to make a consistent conceptual distinction between threatened suicide, attempted suicide, and committed suicide. These strictures make the American *psychological* literature of dubious value. The short account which follows deals with the more formal *psychological* approach and is intended to let the reader catch the flavour of the material for himself. For the reader untrained in psychological techniques this section may present some relative difficulty in relation to the other chapters, due to lack of familiarity with the material presented despite efforts to keep it as simple as possible.

The Rorschach Ink-blot Test, surely one of the most widely known of all psychological instruments, has as its rationale the notion that if a person is given a relatively ambiguous and meaningless stimulus, namely an ink-blot, then he will "project" onto this stimulus his own feelings, desires, ambitions, and so forth. On this assumption has been built an extensive body of theory and practice, to say nothing of a belief in the test which is quite unshaken by report after adverse report in which the reliability and validity* of the test have been shown to be minimal. In the psychodynamically oriented culture in which American clinical psychologists work, the "benefits" of the insights gained through using the Rorschach outweigh such trivia as poor reliability and validity. This cavalier attitude to experimental design is evident in Neuringer's excellent summary of work on suicide involving the Rorschach. He pointed out that most of the contradictory and equivocal results were due to methodological inadequacies and poorly designed studies. From his review of the area, Neuringer concluded that there were no specific Rorschach "signs" of suicide; that is to say, there were no specific projected responses to the ink-blots which were peculiar to the suicide prone. Almost all of the studies surveyed by Neuringer had been retrospective, utilizing test records culled from a variety of files and case notes. The time lag between testing and suicide, in the cases where patients had killed themselves, was often one of years rather than months or days. The use of such varied data, especially when coupled with the omnibus definitions of suicidal behaviour used by many of the researchers, mitigated against the Rorschach producing useful results. Neuringer made a case for suspending judgement on the value of the ink-blot method in

---

* Reliability is when a test measures something in a consistent manner. Validity is when a test measures what it purports to measure.

identifying suicidal behaviour. Certainly its exponents, by their failure to use adequate designs and definitions, have not presented it in a good light. The most distressing feature, however, is a degree of ignorance of the psychiatric literature on suicidal behaviour which is appalling.

The Thematic Apperception Test (TAT), a projective test in which the subject is asked to weave stories around a number of intentionally vague pictures, was devised to provide a means of assessing the needs and influences which determine an individual's behaviour in relation to other people. Since the psycho-social aspects of suicidal behaviour have been widely recognized, it is surprising that the TAT has been used so infrequently. If the Rorschach has been overly popular with researchers, then certainly the TAT has been neglected, although such studies as have been carried out using the TAT indicate that suicidal and non-suicidal individuals are not differentiated. These results led Farberow to put forward some very interesting suggestions. He considered that it would be possible to devise special TAT-like cards which formed a continuum of pictorial stimuli to evoke suicidal fantasies. These cards would range from one which, for almost all normal subjects, would have no suicidal content to a card which would elicit suicidal responses from almost all subjects. This suggestion was an important step forward in projective test methodology relating to suicide, but to date it has remained only a suggestion.

The Minnesota Multiphasic Personality Inventory, better known as the MMPI, enjoys high status in the field of self-administered tests, this status being comparable with that of the Rorschach among projective techniques. First published in the early 1940's, it is in many ways obsolescent, but familiarity and a vast body of empirical data ensure its continued use. This test was originally constructed as an aid to the diagnosis of psychiatric patients and contains 550 items of a very diverse nature. Some report observable behaviour, some reflect inner feelings, some tap general attitudes, while others elicit reports of symptoms of abnormal behaviour. The original scales, eight in all, were made up from items which discriminated certain clinical groups from normals—for example, the hysteria (Hy) scale was one which differentiated clinically diagnosed hysterics from normals. Over the years a great number of scales have been devised, and the psychiatric labels attached to the original eight have become anachronistic, so that currently the scales are referred to by numbers rather than by name. Many psychiatric hospitals and clinics administer the MMPI to every patient, a state of affairs which has facilitated retrospective studies using this test. A wide range of "suicidal" patients have been studied to try to identify an MMPI "suicide profile". This has met with little success. As with the Rorschach, the general level of methodology and design has been poor, definitions of populations studied have all too often been vague, and the researchers' awareness of other literature in the area studied almost completely absent. None of the writers have put forward any clear statement about the relationship between making threats about suicide, actually attempting suicide and dying by suicide. The impression gained is that these three kinds of behaviour form a continuum showing the same pathology in differing degrees. Indeed, one early study used the MMPI protocols of psychiatric patients who had "established suicidal preoccupation" without any history of threats or attempts, and went on to make conclusions about suicide.

To add to this confused state of affairs, all the patients whose MMPI protocols appear in these studies were psychiatric in-patients in veterans' administration hospitals. Patients in the attempted suicide groups had almost all made their attempt prior to their admission to hospital; those forming the threat suicide groups had made these threats while already in-patients. The suicides had all too often died after discharge from hospital, and in many cases the suicide occurred years after the MMPI protocol had been completed. From the work of Cohen and his associates we know that in San Francisco, at least, persons who have attempted suicide are briefly observed in emergency wards; the majority of such patients are promptly discharged without further treatment or follow-up, and only those who are patently very disturbed remain as in-patients. If such hospital practice, which appears to be very similar to British procedure, applies to veterans' administration establishments, then the "attempted suicides" available for MMPI testing are a very selected group indeed.

Early British Studies

The British literature on the psychology of suicidal behaviour is scanty. Apart from our own work in Edinburgh only one other study has been reported. By good fortune this study, by Vinoda, used some of the tests we have used, so that although in some respects her group is not comparable with the Edinburgh populations, being composed of women who were admitted to a psychiatric ward after their suicidal attempt, some points of contact do exist.

In our first study of the personalities of patients admitted to the Poisoning Treatment Centre, the Neuroticism Scale Questionnaire (NSQ) was given to eighty-four individuals who had made a suicidal attempt. The NSQ is a questionnaire designed to screen out relatively neurotic individuals using those personality dimensions which best differentiate normals from persons clinically diagnosed as being neurotic. Each of the dimensions, comprising tendermindedness, depressed mood, submissiveness, and anxiety, is scored separately and the totals are combined to give a total neuroticism score. Compared with the results obtained by normal respondents to the test, the patients produced scores which indicated that they *were very anxious, depressed, and low in their spirits, and generally neurotic.* Considering the main psychiatric diagnostic categories within the patient group only one difference was found—neurotics were more submissive than people with personality disorders. Using two measures of psychiatric symptomatology, the Personal Illness and Character Disorder scales of the Symptom Sign Inventory (SSI), we were able to classify our eighty-four attempted suicides as follows: 56 per cent were classed as character disorders, 32 per cent as psychiatrically ill but not character disorders, and the remaining 12 per cent were classed as normal. Using these same psychiatric scales, Vinoda's patients could be divided up in the following manner: 39 per cent of her attempted suicides were character disorders only, 52 per cent were psychiatrically ill but not character disorders, and 9 per cent were normal. For her first control group of non-suicidal psychiatric patients, the respective percentages were 24 per cent character disordered, 55 per cent ill but not character disordered, and 21 per cent normal. None of the medical or surgical in-patients in her second control group emerged as being character disordered, but 22 per cent showed noticeable signs of psychological disturbance. Allowing for differences in the composition of these groups of attempted suicides, Vinoda's being psychiatric in-patients by virtue of being attempted suicides, while the Edinburgh patients were interviewed before psychiatric screening had been carried out, both studies show that a fair proportion of attempted suicide patients have disorders of character showing interpersonal difficulties, plaintiveness, and self-pity.

An attempt was made to contact our group of patients by post some weeks after they had been seen in hospital and they were asked to fill in the

NSQ and SSI questionnaires again. The high level of anxiety or emotional upset shown by these patients intrigued us—was this a temporary state of affairs, a transient upset related to the attempt or to being in hospital, or was high anxiety with its accompanying feelings of tenseness and apprehensiveness an enduring aspect of the personalities of people who made attempts at suicide? Anxiety can be a *state*—a temporary thing—or it can be a *trait*—an enduring feature of a person's behaviour. Sometimes it can be both together. It was decided to re-test patients to see whether changes in their anxiety and other test scores had taken place. Since it was anticipated that some patients would not respond to our postal re-test the precaution was taken of ascertaining whether those who did respond differed in any way from those who did not respond. Women proved to be better responders than men, 71 per cent of the former replying as opposed to 47 per cent of the latter. This difference in response led us to look at the results for men and women separately. For both sexes responders and non-responders were similar in regard to age, civil state, the method used in their suicidal attempt, the length of time they spent in the Poisoning Treatment Centre, psychiatric diagnosis and disposal, time lag between admission to hospital and postal re-testing, and time lag between discharge from hospital and re-testing. Men who responded to the postal follow-up differed from those who did not on two interesting variables. Not only did they more often have a history of previous suicidal attempts, they more often made suicidal attempts in the 2 years following their key admission. Clearly this group of men who responded to our postal contact remained a disproportionate number of the kind of patient identified as being "repeat prone" in earlier Edinburgh studies. These repeat-prone individuals, while displaying a variety of acute reactions to frustrating circumstances, are characterized mainly by having repeated episodes of, to them, unbearable distress when they resort to impulsive self-poisoning behaviour.

Quite surprisingly, the men who responded to postal re-testing had, while in hospital, scored lower on our anxiety scale than the non-responders. This could have been because they were very anxious prior to their attempt and because the act with its attendant medical treatment and familial empathy served as an anxiety-reducing event. Their re-test scores are only a little higher than their original ones and so there is no way of demonstrating in any definite manner that their anxiety levels do vary to any great extent. Nonetheless, their anxiety level is higher than what would be expected in the population at large. The non-responders showed very high anxiety when tested in hospital, but in the absence of re-test information we cannot determine whether this very high level of emotional upset was a habitual state of affairs or a temporary reaction to events.

In contrast to the men, women who responded to our postal re-test seemed to be fairly representative of all the women in the sample. Accordingly we were able to extrapolate the re-test results to women attempted suicides as a whole. On the more stable and enduring characteristics, assessed by the NSQ, no change at re-test was shown. On the other hand, there was a reduction in scores on both the symptom scales of Personal Illness and Character Disorder. The longer the patients had been out of hospital the greater was the reduction in these scores. These results, based on what was really very limited test material, encouraged us to think that psychological test measures could add appreciably to the picture of the attempted-suicide patient. Earlier studies had covered the psychiatric and social features, of the Edinburgh population, and it was felt that a full-scale psychological description would complement these studies.

The tests chosen for our psychological study fulfilled the following criteria: they were objective, standardized instruments developed within the framework of formal theories of personality, namely those of Foulds and Cattell; a substantial body of data relating to normal and psychiatric patients was available, thus facilitating comparisons between attempted suicides and other groups of people, and they had been used extensively in both clinical work and research by us so that we were well aware of their strengths and weaknesses. Before giving an account of this psychological study it is necessary to give some description of these tests.

Tests Used in the Major Psychological Study

As a method of eliciting information about psychiatric signs and symptoms we chose the SSI devised by Foulds and Hope, the instrument we used in our earlier study. The SSI is closely bound up with Foulds's theory of personality dysfunction and has been much used as a criterion diagnostic measure. Foulds's concern has been to develop measures of traits and attitudes on the one hand, and signs and symptoms on the other, the former differing from the latter in three ways. Traits and attitudes are very common while symptoms and signs are not; the former are essentially egosyntonic while the latter are distressing either to the patient or his intimates; and, lastly, traits—and to a lesser extent attitudes—are relatively enduring while symptoms and signs tend to be transient.

While all eighty items of the SSI were administered to patients in this study, only two scales, those for Personal Disturbance (PD) and Character Disorder (CD), were used. The PD scale comprises twenty items similar to the following paraphrased items:

(1) Are you unable to concentrate properly nowadays?
(2) Do you feel that people are saying things about you which are not true?

High scores on the PD scale distinguish people who experience, or are observed to manifest, difficulty in mutual personal relationships, this difficulty being so distressing to many of them or to their intimates that help is sought to alleviate their problems. This scale is an improved version of the Personal Illness (PI) scale used in our earlier study. Based on the scores obtained by normal subjects and psychiatric patients, the three categories of personal disturbance shown in Table 2 were set up.

TABLE 2. CATEGORIES OF PERSONAL DISTURBANCE

	Normals (%)	Psychiatric patients (%)
Normal (scores of 0 and 1)	90	10
Uncertain (scores of 2, 3, and 4)	10	26
Personally disturbed (scores of 5 and above)	0	64

Using these three categories, the scale would not classify any normals as personally disturbed although 10 per cent of a normal group would fall within the uncertain category. Only 10 per cent of any group of psychiatric patients would be misclassified as "normal" while a further 26 per cent would fall in the uncertain area. We felt that in this study an "uncertain" category of disturbance would be particularly meaningful since patients passing through the Poisoning Treatment Centre frequently have little or no formal psychiatric symptomatology.

The CD scale is a measure which attempts to identify persons who have long-standing neurotic conditions which are marked by chronic inter-personal difficulties, plaintiveness, and the arousal of antipathy in those who treat them. Foulds, in developing this scale, found that when the CD scale was not used in the SSI this group of patients tended to be given diagnoses of psychotic depression, a finding which led him to suggest that the use of this scale would reduce misclassification errors in the SSI.

The second test used, the Hostility and Direction of Hostility Question-naire (HDHQ) devised by Caine, Foulds, and Hope, is designed to measure a wide range of possible manifestations of aggression, hostility, or punitive-ness. The authors of the questionnaire assume that hostility is a unitary entity which can be directed inward on the self or outward against other people or objects. Three subscales, acting-out hostility, criticism of others, and delusional hostility, comprise the measures of *extra-punitive* or outward-directed hostility, while scales of self-criticism and delusional guilt are measures of *intro-punitive* or inward-directed hostility.

The third test, the Sixteen Personality Factor Questionnaire (16PF) of Cattell, aims to provide a much wider coverage of personality traits than those comprising the NSQ used in our first psychological study. The theoretical basis of the 16PF lies in the many publications of Cattell, the simplest account of whose position is to be found in his book *The Scientific Analysis of Personality*. Cattell, more than any other personality theorist, has insisted on the need for a multivariate approach to the problems of analysing personality, and the 16PF is the best-known product of his immense research programme. This insistence on the use of sophisticated statistical analysis, combined with an unfortunate predilection for coining neologisms when identifying personality factors, has reduced the impact of his work, but there is evidence that psychologists are showing increasing appreciation of his contribution to personality assessment.

The 16PF test assesses personality along sixteen primary dimensions or factors which are listed in Table 3. These factors are not completely independent from one another, and it is possible to reduce them to four broad-ranging but less exact secondary dimensions. Of these secondary dimensions one is the anxiety factor found in the NSQ while another is introversion–extraversion.

The second-order factor of anxiety can be considered as a measure of general psychological well-being. Persons scoring low on anxiety scales

TABLE 3. BRIEF DESCRIPTION OF THE 16PF FACTORS

Factor	Low score	High score
A	Aloof	Outgoing
B	Unintelligent	Intelligent
C	Emotionally unstable	Mature, stable
E	Submissive	Dominant
F	Reticent	Enthusiastic
G	Expedient	Conscientious
H	Shy	Venturesome
I	Tough-minded	Sensitive
L	Trustful	Suspecting
M	Practical	Self-absorbed
N	Simple	Sophisticated
O	Confident	Apprehensive
Q1	Conservative	Radical
Q2	Group dependent	Self-sufficient
Q3	Uncontrolled	Self-controlled
Q4	Relaxed	Tense

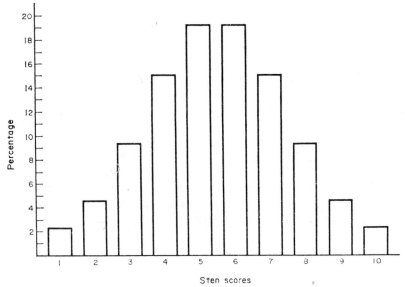

FIG. 3. Percentage of people falling in each sten score.

C

tend to find their lives generally satisfying and feel able to achieve their particular goals, while those persons who are high scorers on anxiety tend to find life less rewarding and tend to be dissatisfied with their lot. The introversion–extraversion scale contrasts the person who is rather shy and retiring in social situations with the person who is uninhibited in thought and deed and is usually to the fore in social activities.

In order to facilitate the comparisons of scores obtained on the various scales, the raw scores on each scale are transformed into a standard ten-point scale, usually referred to as a *sten scale*. Figure 3 shows how in a normal group of people the most frequent sten scores are those of 5 and 6, stens of 4 and 7 are slightly less common, and so forth, until it is seen that stens of 1 and 10 are very rare in normal people.

Both the 16PF and the HDHQ are non-projective questionnaire methods of assessing personality in which a person's responses are taken at face value. It is always possible that such tests can be distorted by persons who want to paint a very good or very bad picture of themselves. Psychologists have hotly debated the issues of the social desirability of various items and the presence or absence of various response "sets", such as always saying "yes" to questions regardless of their content. One of the skills involved in clinical practice is that of eliciting the active co-operation of the patient, and there is no reason to doubt that the majority of patients are well motivated to be co-operative and truthful in their response to questionnaires and inventories, particularly when they perceive the tester as part of a team responding to a call for help.

Fifty men and fifty women admitted to the Poisoning Treatment Centre were tested. These patients were all interviewed by psychiatrists and were considered to have made suicide attempts. As soon as their physical condition allowed, usually between 12 and 48 hours after admission, they were interviewed, completed the SSI with the psychologist, and then filled in the HDHQ and the 16PF under supervision. On the basis of these test results we can present a description of the group as a whole before going on to look for distinctive subgroups of patients.

Degree of Psychiatric Disturbance

On the basis of their responses to the SSI *almost half of the patients (48 per cent), men and women alike, emerged as being character disordered.* In such a group one would expect to find much evidence of chronic interpersonal difficulties, plaintiveness, and self-pity. *A further 40 per cent showed signs of psychiatric disturbance other than character disorder,* half being personally disturbed and half showing uncertain pathology. The remaining *12 per cent showed no signs of psychiatric pathology* on the SSI. These proportions are indistinguishable from the findings we obtained 2 years earlier.

The results of testing on the HDHQ show that as a group our attempted suicide patients score higher on both intro-punitive and extra-punitive aspects of hostility than do normal subjects or neurotic patients. On the same test Vinoda found similar differences between her normals, neurotics, and attempted suicides. It can be said from these results that while attempted suicides are every bit as self-critical and guilt-ridden as psychiatric patients, *they are more prone to act out and to be critical and suspicious of other folk.* The results on the 16PF confirmed and spelled out in more detail the high level of anxiety shown by attempted suicides in our earlier study. Emotional immaturity and instability, apprehensiveness, suspiciousness, and low frustration tolerance all combine to give these high overall scores on anxiety. Cattell thinks of anxiety as a disorganizing force or symptom of disorganization rather than as a drive or motivating force. From the description he gives of the anxious person, showing, on the one hand, irritability, suspicion of others, and tenseness, and, on the other, lack of confidence, dependency, and a sense of guilt and worthlessness, it is clear that anxiety as used in the 16PF and NSQ represents much more than "butterflies in the stomach". The attempted suicide who has a high anxiety level is in a state of emotional upset which must affect his sense of judgement, his ability to plan adequately, and his reactions to events going on around him. The results from our earlier study give us reason to believe that in this population of attempted suicides *such a state of emotional upset is no transient thing,* rather it appears to be enduring and persistent. Looking at groups of attempted suicides, psychiatric patients, and normals who have completed the 16PF, it is found that about 15 out of every 100 normals could be labelled "anxious personality profile", while twice as many psychiatric patients would be so classed. For attempted suicides the "anxious personality profile" accounts for half of the group; in other words, the person showing severe emotional upset is found three times more often in the latter group than in a group of normal people. The attempted suicides' *poor frustration tolerance, tenseness, and fearfulness* are not confined to their psychological test performance:

they are only too evident in their clinical and social histories. What has been described by the clinicians as impulsive behaviour can be explained by this feature of general emotional upset.

While emotional upset is the outstanding characteristic of our attempted-suicide patients, tending to dwarf other features of their personalities, it can be seen that these patients are somewhat more introverted and lacking in social conscience than normal people. The introverted behaviour shown by these patients is of a kind indicating that they are *temperamentally independent, aloof and suspicious of other people's motives.* Most psychiatrically ill groups, especially neurotics, are more introverted than normal persons because they are more submissive, restrained, and introspective; indeed, these trait features are used in Cattell's NSQ just because they discriminate neurotics from normals. Our attempted suicides tend not to display this particular pattern of introverted behaviour. Their withdrawal from interpersonal contacts is best seen in the light of *their lack of social conscience*; they are aloof not through shyness or self-sufficiency but through *their disregard for group mores and conventions.* Again, this test finding is consistent with the finding that social withdrawal frequently takes the form of leaving home or seeking escape from contact with people through drugs.

Just as clinically there is no "suicidal personality", so also is there no unique psychological test profile for persons who attempt suicide. As has been demonstrated, impulsiveness and poor interpersonal relationships, high anxiety, and hostility are common in attempted suicide, but they are not ubiquitous, nor are such characteristics confined to this particular population. One of the aims in this study, therefore, was to search for personality differences *within* our group of attempted suicides, hoping thereby to distinguish groups of persons with similar characteristics which could be used to predict better or worse social prognosis. To further this aim a number of comparisons were made within the group, making these for men and women separately.

Major Personality Features of the Group

Attention was paid to various aspects of the psychiatric state of the patients: the major psychiatric diagnoses, the results of the SSI, and three rating scales in which an attempt was made to assess separately the presence or otherwise of symptoms, personality abnormalities, and social deviance.

These rating scales were used because it had been noted in earlier studies that most of the clinical diagnoses were based not only on signs and symptoms of illness but also on the personality characteristics of the patients. In these earlier studies we also became convinced that some measure of social pathology would be of use as an aid to the more accurate diagnosis of patients seen in the Poisoning Treatment Centre. Accordingly, these three simple rating scales were set up as a first step towards a procedure where a diagnosis could be made based on symptoms, personality abnormality, and social deviance. In the first scale the psychiatrist was asked to indicate the presence or absence of signs and symptoms of *any* psychiatric illness, using the diagnostic approach of Mayer-Gross, Slater, and Roth. The rated presence of personality abnormality and social deviance depended only on the opinion of the psychiatrists, although it was suggested to them that the range of behaviour commonly seen in general medical and surgical patients should be used as a baseline against which to rate the patients seen in the Poisoning Treatment Centre.

Degree of life endangerment and whether or not precautions have been taken to avoid or ensure discovery are areas which feature often in the literature on attempted suicide. These were dealt with earlier, and clearly some examination of these topics was necessary in the study now reported. The life-endangerment scale measured the degree to which, in the opinion of the psychiatrist, the patient would have been certain to die if he or she had not been discovered. Similarly, the precaution scale quantified the psychiatrist's judgement as to whether precautions had been taken to avoid discovery or to ensure discovery.

Differences Within the Group

A third area of interest was to attempt to relate personality traits with social factors found in earlier studies to be important in predicting future adjustment. A history of previous suicidal attempts is known to carry implications for future adjustment and was a logical choice for making comparisons within the group. An index of social prognosis was also devised, based on the results of an earlier social follow-up study. The results of that study were carefully examined for items which had been found to be related to the social improvement of attempted suicide patients. Following this examination, lists of important factors were devised for

men and women separately. For women, sixteen items were selected, while
for men the number was fifteen; many items applied to both sexes. For
women the following items, if present, carried good prognostic implications:

> Patient unmarried, aged under 34 years.
> Extant marriage, patient aged 35 years or over, or married for 5 years
> or more.
> Patient living in own home (if married) or with parents (if single).
> Use of aspirin (salicylates) as a method of self-poisoning.
> Primary diagnosis of "no psychiatric illness".

The following items, if present, carried poor prognostic implications:

> Patient unmarried, aged 34 years or over.
> Extant marriage with violence, infidelity, alcoholism in the spouse or
> with marital disharmony as a precipitant.
> Patient separated or divorced.
> Patient's work record one of frequent job changes (3 + in year),
> unemployment, or casual labour.
> Patient's social class IV or V (Registrar-General's Classification).
> Drinking or drug taking seen to be a problem by patient, informant,
> or psychiatrist.
> Trouble with the law (any of these: warned by police, approved
> school, probation, fines, jail).
> Use of unusual methods such as cutting, slashing, etc.
> Rating of 1 or 2 on life-endangerment scale.
> Personality disorder as main diagnosis.
> History of previous suicidal attempt.

For men the following items carried good implications for social improvement:

> Patient unmarried, aged under 20 years.
> Extant marriage, patient aged 35 years or over, or married for 5 or
> more years.
> Patient living in own home (if married) or with parents (if single).

Use of aspirin (salycilates) as a method of self-poisoning.
Neurosis or depression as a main diagnosis.

The presence of the remaining items implied poor social improvement:

Patient unmarried, aged 20 years or more.
Extant marriage with violence, infidelity, alcoholism in spouse or with marital disharmony as a precipitant.
Patient separated or divorced.
Patient's work record one of frequent job changes (3 + in year), unemployment, or casual labour.
Drinking or drug taking seen to be a problem by patient, informant, or psychiatrist.
Trouble with the law (any of these: warned by police, approved school, probation, fines, jail).
Use of unusual methods such as cutting, slashing, etc.
Rating of 1 or 2 on life-endangerment scale.
Personality disorder or "nil psychiatric" as main diagnosis.
History of previous suicidal attempts.

In discussing the results of these within-group comparisons it might be easier for the reader if each group of psychological variables is considered in turn to see which, if any, of the comparisons produced differences on these social items. The psychological variables are best considered under four headings, anxiety and its associated primary factors, introversion-extraversion and its associated primary factors, other 16PF factors, and the HDHQ. It should be remembered that men showed no differences when rated for symptoms and signs of illness and produced one difference of doubtful significance on the social prognosis index. No differences were found for women on the rating scales of life endangerment, precautions taken, or personality abnormality.

ANXIETY

For men differences on anxiety were found between SSI categories and on the rating of social deviance. On the former, character-disordered patients are much more anxious than normals, their anxiety being characterized by apprehensiveness, guilt proneness, excitability, and tenseness. Men rated as being socially disordered are also characterized by apprehensiveness and guilt proneness but are, in addition, low in frustration tolerance, tend to be unrealistic in their thinking, and are prone to follow their whims and fancies of the moment. Thus while anxiety is a feature of both the character-disordered person and the patient rated as socially disordered, it is manifested in rather different ways in these two categories. The excitability and tenseness shown by character disorders are also shown by those patients rated by the psychiatrists as having taken precautions to ensure their discovery.

Women showed differences in anxiety when considered according to clinical diagnosis, SSI categories, and history of previous suicidal behaviour. Clinically diagnosed personality disorders are more anxious than those suffering from depressive disorders, manifesting such features as immaturity and emotional instability, being mistrustful, easily made apprehensive and restless. Of all the primary factors associated with anxiety only social inhibition and lack of self-control fail to show differences between these diagnostic groups, who do not therefore differ on what might be termed the "social withdrawal" aspect of anxiety. The picture presented here is of an overabundance of motor energy which has no adequate mode of discharge. Clearly the potential for impulsive behaviour in such persons must be considerable. Women categorized as normal or "uncertain" on the SSI are much less anxious than those deemed personally disturbed. The uncertain or borderline group are very similar to normals in their levels of apprehensiveness and tenseness but differ on factor H, appearing to be more socially withdrawing. Normals are distinguished from the personally disturbed group on all the primary anxiety factors. Women who have made a suicidal attempt at some time in the past are more anxious than non-repeaters, being very easily upset and emotionally unstable as well as displaying a tendency to worry and brood about the future. The presence of a history of previous attempts as an item in the social prognosis index probably accounts for the fact that some differences in anxiety occur between groups classified on the index.

Anxiety, or some of the primary factors which contribute to it, is clearly an important personality dimension in the women tested although it discriminates men less well. Primary factors C and O (see Table 3) show differences on most of the comparisons made, and a more detailed account of them seems to be called for. Factor C according to Cattell is essentially a trait of emotional integration, a measure of the extent to which impulses are controlled and expressed in the pursuit of long-term goals. Cattell suggests that this trait is largely determined by early environmental factors, and reports that background variables associated with low C scores include parental disharmony, either conflict or actual separation, emotional, over-protective mothering, and histories of truancy or delinquency. Persons low in C are dissatisfied, tend to be excessively emotional when frustrated, and constantly complain about ill health and lack of energy. Factor O is considered by Cattell to be a dispositional trait, found in most psychiatric groups, and best characterized by guilt proneness. The combination of these two factors gives us a *picture of a woman who is a chronic complainer, dissatisfied with her lot, and while prone to be extremely emotional is also full of guilt and apprehension. Such a woman has a poor social prognosis, tends to be a repeater, and while producing a wealth of symptomatology is most likely to be diagnosed a personality disorder.*

INTROVERSION–EXTRAVERSION

For both men and women the introversion–extraversion dimension yields differences between those patients rated as markedly socially deviant and those given low ratings on that scale, but the direction of the differences differs in the sexes. Men rated as having no social disorder score fairly average on introversion–extraversion, with middling scores on factors reflecting social participation, happy-go-lucky nature, and self-sufficiency; the middle group tend to be somewhat extraverted, sociable, and clearly able to relate to people, while those considered to be socially disordered or deviant manifest their introverted nature by being rather detached from people, taciturn, and temperamentally independent. The aspects of intro-version–extraversion which do not differentiate the groups are those relating to dominance and shyness.

Women rated as having some features of social disorder are very intro-verted, fairly reticent, and very shy and timid. Women at the extremes of this factor, showing the least and the most social disorder, are average on introversion–extraversion as a whole although the most disordered group are markedly more dominant and aggressive than the other groups.

For men the rating of social disorder and deviance produces differences on both second-order dimensions of the 16PF. Men with no social disorder are average on both factors, men who are clearly socially deviant *are both anxious and introverted in a way which suggests that they are "loners", paying little heed to the needs and expectations of other people.* The middle group, who have some degree of deviance, show some of the apprehensiveness and guilt proneness associated with high anxiety but are temperamentally more stable and appear to be able to relate well to people. Women who are socially deviant are more dominant and aggressive than non-deviant women, *so that if the men in this category are "loners" the women appear to be "harridans".*

OTHER 16PF FACTORS

Of the remaining 16PF factors, B, G, I, M, N, and Q1, only G (conscientiousness) yields more than one significant difference within groups, both differences occurring among men. Clinically diagnosed personality disorders are less conscientious and imbued with a sense of duty than are depressive disorders, while men rated as socially disordered are similarly differentiated from those not so rated. Cattell is not very explicit about the meaning of this factor but assigns to it *some of the characteristics of super-ego.* It seems to measure at its low end a *disregard for conventional morality and an unwillingness to accede to cultural demands,* traits which add to the picture of the socially deviant male as a loner. G is the only 16PF factor which shows differences between the major diagnostic categories of men; this is an unexceptionable finding.

HOSTILITY

Finally, let us look at the results relating to hostility. There are differences for men within SSI categories and ratings of personality abnormality on general hostility. On the SSI, character disorders in particular score very high on both intro-punitive and extra-punitive dimensions. It is likely that this amount of emotional upset reflected in the HDHQ is related to the high scores on second-order anxiety shown by these same patients. Men rated as having *abnormal personalities* are not different from the rest on the 16PF but they do have very high scores on general hostility and differ from those rated as not abnormal on extra-punitiveness, indicating a marked bias towards *aggressive modes of expression.* Significant differences on acting-out hostility and criticism of others, two of the subtests contributing to this measure, indicate that this extra-punitiveness *carries possible physical as well as verbal connotations.*

Like men, women vary on general hostility when viewed in terms of the SSI categories, but they tend to express such hostility in a more intro-punitive, self-critical, and guilt-ridden manner. Women with personality disorders score much higher on hostility than women suffering from depressive disorders; there are differences on all the subscales except self-criticism. In both these instances, SSI categories and clinical diagnosis, differences in second-order anxiety and its associated first-order factors of the 16PF have been prominent.

For men, many of the within-group comparisons yield differences on the extra-punitive side of the HDHQ. Very extra-punitive men tend to be rated high on personality abnormality and social disorder, tend to score at the "high risk of death" end of the life-endangerment scale, and are more likely to be diagnosed as personality disorders rather than depressive disorders.

Women tend to differ on intro-punitiveness. As already stated, character disorders and personally disturbed women are more intro-punitive than SSI normals or the borderline disturbed. Women with a history of a previous suicidal attempt are also more intro-punitive than non-repeaters.

In general the HDHQ results tie in with the 16PF, especially where anxiety and general hostility are found together. An interesting sex difference is that men tend to vary in the amount of extra-punitiveness they display while women tend to vary most on intro-punitiveness.

Personality Types Emerging from the Study

One male personality type in a group of attempted suicides seems to be characterized by emotional instability, apprehensiveness and poor self-control, a marked tendency to be self-sufficient, and a poorly developed social conscience. Since men as a group are high on general hostility and extra-punitiveness it is probable that this type is extra-punitive in relation to normal men. A synthesis of these trait descriptions indicates that *this type of person is a "loner" who pays little heed to the needs and expectations of society, experiences little desire for close personal contacts, is emotionally volatile, and is prone to be extra-punitive.* Such a synthesis has a striking resemblance to the McCords' criteria of psychopathy.

The second-order factor of anxiety which distinguishes women who have attempted suicide from other groups of women also distinguishes within the group. One type which emerges is that of a woman *who is emotionally labile and impulsive, complains about lack of energy, is dissatisfied with life, and tends to be apprehensive and guilt prone. Despite producing a wealth of symptomatology she tends to be diagnosed a personality disorder and has a poor social prognosis.* This type of woman is close to Foulds's concept of the character-disordered individual.

For both sexes it would appear that important subgroups can be identified on the basis of certain personality traits. These subgroups are clearly *forms of personality disorder* which in men takes the form of sociopathy and in women takes the shape of character disorder. In a sense, patients scoring like these types are those of the population studied who are most *unlike* normals; the men are the most anxious, most introverted, and most lacking in social conscience; while the women are the most anxious, apprehensive, and guilt prone. Other types are almost certainly present; there is evidence for a type of male patient who is very character disordered, with little control over his impulses, and who shows a great deal of tenseness and energy potential. This type is rather similar to the character-disordered type of woman. Similarly, some women, described here as "harridans", seem to have a close resemblance to the male socio-pathic type. These types occur with less frequency than the former subgroups, and many more patients would have to be studied to spell out in detail the salient psychological characteristics of such persons.

CHAPTER 4

Ecological Correlates of Suicidal Behaviour

Brief Description of the Ecological Method

Studies which have attempted to relate sickness of all kinds to social and environmental factors are numerous. In particular the importance of the social setting in the development and recognition of behaviours such as attempted suicide and completed suicide has long been recognized. Very early in the research programme into suicidal behaviour in Edinburgh it became apparent that some areas of the city contributed more than their share of admissions to the Poisoning Treatment Centre. Areas having high, moderately high, moderately low, and low prevalence rates for suicidal behaviour were identified, and these rates were compared with rates for overcrowding, family dislocation, where known criminals resided, single-person households, and proportion of people living in hotels. The latter two variables, aimed at assessing social isolation, *did not* relate to self-poisoning; the other variables, whose aim was to reflect social disorganization, *did* relate to suicidal behaviour. These and other findings led us to look further at ecological aspects of the citizens of Edinburgh, in particular those citizens who attempted or committed suicide.

The ecological approach to research involves techniques which many readers will find novel. Accordingly the techniques involved in the collection and analysis of our data as well as the findings will be described briefly. It is important for people to be able to distinguish between data gathered from individual persons and data gathered from geographical areas. Every large community is a patchwork of many diverse areas each of which has its own type of people, activities, physical characteristics, life styles, and traditions; in brief, its own sub-culture. The investigation and analysis of such variations have in the past shed useful light on deviant behaviour, mental disorder, and physical illness. The most common area units which

65

have been studied have been population census tracts or the electoral wards of cities. Provided there is a fair amount of variation *between* tracts or wards and a degree of uniformity or lack of variation *within* these tracts or wards, it is usually profitable to analyse data in this ecological fashion. These analyses provide information on some of the structural properties of cities and their constituent wards. Every major city is relatively unique in its structure, and the ecological analysis of problems in any one city must be viewed *essentially as a case description*. In addition it must always be remembered that ecological correlations may be suggestive of individual correlations but *the two must not be mistaken for each other*. The main value of correlations between variables analysed by the ecological method is to facilitate the formulation of hypotheses which can and must be tested out by other means.

By good fortune the city of Edinburgh has developed in such a way as to make ecological research particularly worth while. Of its twenty-three electoral wards (Fig. 4) the first three, in numerical order, encompass the

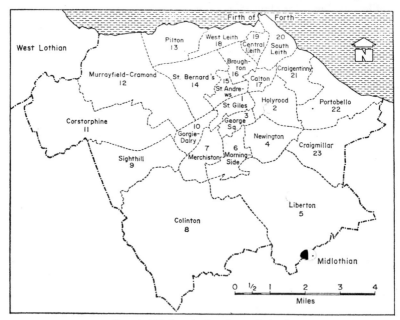

FIG. 4. Edinburgh city electoral wards.

centuries-old, multi-storied buildings of the Royal Mile. In these wards are to be found Edinburgh Castle and Her Majesty's Palace of Holyroodhouse in close proximity to numerous less desirable premises, lodging houses, and cheap hostels. Wards 15–20 extend north-eastward from the city centre to the Firth of Forth and the port of Leith; for the most part this area comprises nineteenth-century industrial tenement buildings. Immediately to the south and west of the city centre lies an inner ring of spacious, old-established dwellings, traditional homes of Edinburgh's well-to-do professional workers. An outer ring of more recent buildings of modest amenity and undistinguished architecture completes the city. Three of these outer wards are marked by being predominantly local authority housing schemes, the others comprise areas where owner-occupied houses predominate. Slum clearance over the past three decades has left the central wards with steadily declining populations, very little new building having taken the place of the old. Two wards, 1 and 23, have a special relationship. The latter ward, on the south-east perimeter of the city, has as its core a 1930 housing scheme populated by families moved *en bloc* from the slums of the central ward. Although removed forcibly from their old habitations, many of these families took with them their characteristic way of life.

Such has been Edinburgh's pattern of development that most of these electoral wards show differences between one another while having a fair degree of uniformity within themselves. Utilizing this favourable situation it was possible to compare the distribution of suicidal behaviour in various parts of the city with a large variety of social information, most of which was readily available from census tables and the reports of various departments of the local authority. Much information which is useful for this kind of study is annually collected and reported from all sorts of sources and is generally accessible to most researchers at little cost in terms of time and money.

Variables Used in the Ecological Study

Table 4 gives a list of the variables used and the sources from which they were obtained.

The first step in treating these variables was as follows. Rates of incidence for every 1000 units at risk were calculated for each of the twenty-three electoral wards of the city. For instance, in each ward the number of owner-

occupier houses was divided by the total number of dwelling houses in
that ward and the result expressed as a rate per 1000 houses. On the basis
of these rates the wards were placed in rank order for each variable, the
ward with the highest rate being given a rank of 1 and that with the lowest

TABLE 4. SOCIAL VARIABLES USED AND SOURCE OF INFORMATION

Overcrowding (over 1·5 persons per room)
Local-authority-owned houses
Owner-occupier houses
Rented, unfurnished houses
Rented, furnished accommodation
One-person dwellings
Density of population   } All from the census
Old-age pensioners
Visitors from outside Scotland
Commonwealth and Irish residents
Resident aliens
Divorced persons

Valuation assessment of property
Children taken into care
Eviction notices
Final warnings about rent arrears
Rent arrears
Persistent truancy   All from Edinburgh
Infant mortality   Corporation departments
Stillbirths
Road fatalities
Road accidents (persons involved)
Road accidents (site)
Suicide

Three indices of telephone vandalism   GPO Edinburgh

Juvenile delinquency   Jackson private communication

Cruelty to children   Royal Scottish Society for
                                              Prevention of Cruelty to
                                              Children

Adolescent psychiatric referrals
Adolescent attempted suicide   } Data from our own files
All ages attempted suicide
Repeat attempted suicide

rate a rank of 23. Once ranked, each variable was then correlated with every other variable using Spearman rank order correlation coefficients.

Each of these correlation coefficients indicates the degree of association between a pair of variables, and if a table containing all the correlations existing between our thirty-one variables were set out it would have 465 such associations to study. Clearly it is necessary to apply to the table of correlations some procedure which will make easier the task of comprehending the *patterns* of relationships indicated by the correlations.

Analysing the Data—Example of a Typal Method

The method put forward here is a method of analysing variables into types proposed by McQuitty. This method of analysis works on the basic principle that every member of a type is more like some other member of that type than any member of any other type. The particular typal method about to be used, Elementary Linkage Analysis (ELA), defines the linkage between two items as being the largest correlation which a variable has with any of the other variables being studied. Thus every variable is assigned to a cluster or group in terms of its highest correlation.

TABLE 5. CORRELATIONS BETWEEN A NUMBER OF SUBJECTS

		1	2	3	4	5	6	7
Politics	1		*0·77*	0·40	0·36	0·01	0·55	0·31
Sociology	2	*0·77*		0·30	0·25	0·10	*0·60*	0·29
Psychology	3	0·40	0·30		*0·65*	*0·50*	0·10	0·17
Economics	4	0·36	0·25	*0·65*		0·45	0·20	0·30
Human growth and development	5	0·01	0·10	0·50	0·45		0·26	0·20
Research methods	6	0·55	0·60	0·10	0·20	0·26		*0·35*
Social policy	7	0·31	0·29	0·17	0·30	0·20	0·35	

As an example of how ELA works, consider Table 5. A number of subjects have been compared by social work teachers and the similarities between pairs of subjects are represented by the correlations in the table. The analysis of this data consists of five steps:

Suicidal Behaviour

1. Underline the highest entry in each *column* of the matrix. (In the table these entries are in *italics*.)
2. Select the highest entry of the entire matrix; the two variables having this correlation constitute the first two variables of the first cluster.
3. Select all those variables which are most like the variables of the first cluster. Do this by reading along the *rows* of the variables which emerged in step 2 and select any italic coefficients in these rows.
4. Select any variables which are most like the variables elicited in step 3. Repeat the procedure of step 3 until no further variables emerge.
5. Excluding all those variables which fall within the first cluster, repeat steps 2–4.

Results of Typal Analysis in the Study

In our subject example two clusters emerge and are shown in Fig. 5. Subjects 1 (politics) and 2 (sociology) form the first pair; research methods

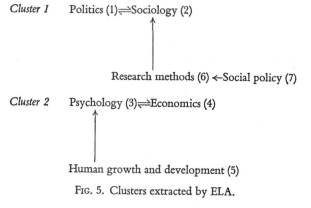

Cluster 1   Politics (1)⇌Sociology (2)

Research methods (6) ←Social policy (7)

Cluster 2   Psychology (3)⇌Economics (4)

Human growth and development (5)

Fig. 5. Clusters extracted by ELA.

(6) joins this cluster because its greatest similarity is with sociology. Social policy (7) also joins this cluster; its greatest association is with research methods. Since no correlations are underlined in row 7, this cluster is complete. Psychology and economics, numbers 3 and 4, have the highest remaining correlations and form the nucleus of cluster 2. Human growth and development (5) has its highest association with psychology and in joining cluster 2 completes the analysis.

Applying this system of analysis to the Edinburgh correlation matrix of social variables, six clusters emerge. These are shown in Fig. 6. Cluster 1 relates eviction notices, rent arrears, and final warnings about rent arrears. The reader might find some confidence in the method of linkage analysis from the variables which go together here, since logically they belong together.

Cluster 2 relates types of accommodation, showing a typical city-centre situation. Where there are few local authority houses and, incidentally, few owner-occupied houses, one is left with buildings which are mainly old tenement properties, often comprising flats of only one or two rooms, and in these densely populated areas one finds many old people, divorced persons, and persons living alone.

Cluster 3 is one specific to the vandalism figures given us by the General Post Office. In passing, it might be noted that it is those areas with fewest telephone boxes which have the highest rates of telephone box vandalism.

Cluster 4 brings together two of the variables which were selected so that some comparison could be made with Sainsbury's earlier study of suicide in London.

Cluster 5 is an important and striking association of items. The reader will by now have appreciated from earlier chapters that persons indulging

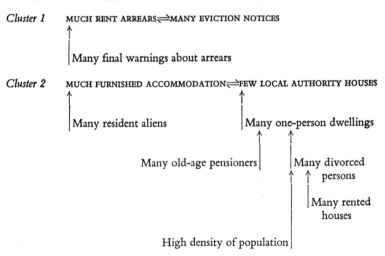

FIG. 6. Linkage analysis of Edinburgh social variables (*continued on page 72*).

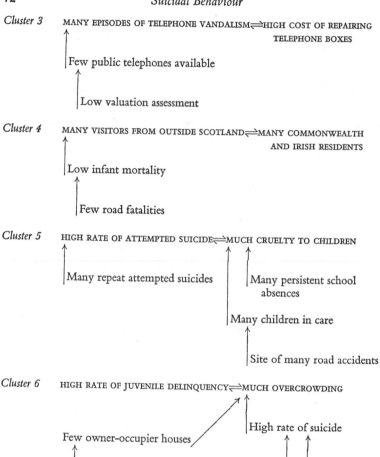

Cluster 3   MANY EPISODES OF TELEPHONE VANDALISM⇌HIGH COST OF REPAIRING
TELEPHONE BOXES

Few public telephones available

Low valuation assessment

Cluster 4   MANY VISITORS FROM OUTSIDE SCOTLAND⇌MANY COMMONWEALTH
AND IRISH RESIDENTS

Low infant mortality

Few road fatalities

Cluster 5   HIGH RATE OF ATTEMPTED SUICIDE⇌MUCH CRUELTY TO CHILDREN

Many repeat attempted suicides

Many persistent school
absences

Many children in care

Site of many road accidents

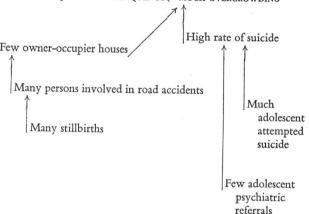

Cluster 6   HIGH RATE OF JUVENILE DELINQUENCY⇌MUCH OVERCROWDING

High rate of suicide

Few owner-occupier houses

Many persons involved in road accidents

Much
adolescent
attempted
suicide

Many stillbirths

Few adolescent
psychiatric
referrals

in suicidal behaviour have appalling difficulties in their interpersonal relationships. This cluster reflects these relationships as identified by an ecological technique and highlights a particular facet of these difficulties. High rates for attempted suicide are related to high rates of cruelty to children, high rates for children being taken into care of the local authority and high rates of school absences through persistent truancy.

Cluster 6 relates rates of delinquency with overcrowding—a state of affairs found by virtually everyone who has studied delinquency. In the areas of the city where overcrowding is great, there the suicide rate is highest.

Social Variables Related to Suicidal Behaviour

ELA uses only some of the information in a correlation matrix; it concentrates on the highest associations between variables. Clearly, then, in any table of associations, there will be many significant correlations between items which cut across clusters. For example, the adolescent attempted-suicide rate correlates highly with that for all attempted suicide, the latter in turn correlating very highly indeed with rates for juvenile delinquency and completed suicide. Accordingly, Table 6 tabulates all the statistically significant relationships which our social variables have with three main kinds of suicidal behaviour: *attempted suicide, repeated attempted suicide, and completed suicide*. Statistically significant correlations are those which would occur by chance less than 5 times in 100; where the odds against a chance association increase to 1 in 100 and 1 in 1000, the terms "high" and "very high" have been used to describe these associations.

Social Variables Manifested by Individuals

Five social variables have significant correlations with all three suicidal behaviours: they are *juvenile delinquency, children taken into care, overcrowding, referrals to the RSSPCC, and divorce*. Where the rates for suicidal behaviour are high, then the rates for these other variables will be high also. Ecological data, although it can point to possible relationships between variables, cannot determine whether these variables occur together in the same individual. A correlation in the ecological setting comes about when the rates of incidence for a pair of variables vary in a like way from ward to ward.

Suicidal Behaviour

TABLE 6. SOCIAL VARIABLES RELATED TO SUICIDAL BEHAVIOUR

Attempted suicide	Repeated attempted suicide	Suicide
Significant correlations ($p < 0.05$)		
Low rates of adolescent psychiatric referral High rates of adolescent attempted suicide High density of population Frequent site of road accidents	Much overcrowding High rate of suicide	High rate of children taken into care Frequent persistent school absences Few owner-occupier houses Many rented tenement houses High rate of repeated attempted suicide High density of population
High, significant correlations ($p < 0.01$)		
Frequent persistent school absences Much rented accommodation Many divorced persons	High rates of juvenile delinquency Much cruelty to children Many divorced persons	Low rate of adolescent psychiatric referral High rate of adolescent attempted suicide High rate of juvenile delinquency Much cruelty to children Many divorced persons
Very high, significant correlation ($p < 0.001$)		
High rates of juvenile delinquency High rate of children taken into care Much overcrowding Much cruelty to children High rate of repeated attempted suicide High rate of suicide	High rate of attempted suicide High rate of children taken into care	High rate of attempted suicide Much overcrowding

These rates could be based on the behaviour of the same people in that people who did X also did Y, or on different people, so that in any ward the people who did X were not the persons who did Y. In each case the ecological correlation would be the same. To find out about correlations for persons it is necessary to investigate individuals—not geographical units. Having access to a large population of people who attempt suicide, it was possible to investigate in individuals the kind of social variables found to be significantly correlated with attempted suicide at an ecological level.

Consider again cluster 5 in Fig. 6. This cluster indicates some association between attempted suicide and what could be called a peculiar parent–child relationship, this relationship being manifested at an ecological level by correlations between the incidence of children who were persistent truants, the incidence of children being taken into the care of the local authority, and the frequency with which the RSSPCC had to take action regarding cases of cruelty to children. In dealing with individual persons we were concerned to find out whether people who had attempted suicide manifested these other variables. Had they been taken into care? Had they been seen by the RSSPCC? Had they been persistent school absentees? The reader will remember the case of the White family (p. 15), which appeared to demonstrate that deviances in behaviour are transmitted through the generations. Since we were investigating ecological correlates which might shed further light on this it became important not only to investigate these variables in our patients but also in their children.

Over a period of 6 weeks ninety-five patients admitted to the Poisoning Treatment Centre following a suicidal attempt were interviewed with regard to a number of the variables suggested by the ecological findings. It was asked: Had the patient had a previous episode of suicidal behaviour? Was his home his own or was it rented and was his family overcrowded? Was he divorced or separated? Had he or any of his children been in trouble with the law, absent from school, taken into care, or had contact with the "cruelty man"? On the basis of the response of these patients to our questions we were able to calculate rates of occurrence for these variables. By comparing these rates with those of other, non-suicidal groups or with other available rates, we determined whether factors which correlated with attempted suicide at the ecological level were found more often in a group of individuals who had attempted suicide than would be expected by chance alone. These rates and their sources are shown in Table 7.

For some of the rates of incidence we were able to use information from the 1966 census; for other rates we used information available from a non-suicidal group who were interviewed as part of another study. However,

Suicidal Behaviour

TABLE 7. RATES OF OCCURRENCE OF CERTAIN VARIABLES
FOR ATTEMPTED SUICIDES AND OTHERS

	Rate per thousand for attempted suicides	Rate per thousand for Edinburgh	Source of comparative data
Overcrowding	294·7	93·0	1966 census
Rented accommodation	389·5	192·6	1966 census
Divorce	73·7	9·7	1966 census
Separation	94·7	25·3	Own data files
Persistent truancy	684·2	2·1	Annual rates for Edinburgh
Court prosecutions	410·5	39·6	Annual rates for Edinburgh
Children in care	200·0	3·4	Annual rates for Edinburgh
RSSPCC	105·3	6·6	Annual rates for Edinburgh
Repeated attempted suicide	442·1	0·5	Annual rates for Edinburgh

for some of the rates, which were partial lifetime rates, it was not possible to present adequate comparative data other than the annual rates of incidence for the city of Edinburgh. It was found that the patients, as children, had seldom been in care or referred to the RSSPCC on more than one occasion, so that the discrepancy between an annual rate and a lifetime rate for these variables might be expected to be small compared with the discrepancies found here. Even if the annual rates for these two variables were multiplied tenfold to give a generous estimate of lifetime rates, they would still be much lower than the rates shown by these attempted-suicide patients. Despite the lack of completely comparable data, the figures shown in Table 7 make it possible to conclude that the variables which ecologically are present to excess in areas where attempted suicide is common are also present to excess in groups of individuals who have attempted suicide.

Of the persons we interviewed in the Poisoning Treatment Centre, forty-four had children, and Table 8 shows the rates of incidence these children had for delinquency, being taken into care, being persistently absent from school, and having contact with the RSSPCC. Two points are worth noting when looking at these rates for children. Regarding persistent truancy, the reader should remember that the peak ages for attempted suicide among women is in the late twenties, so that in many cases families

TABLE 8. RATES OF OCCURRENCES OF CERTAIN VARIABLES
FOR CHILDREN OF ATTEMPTED SUICIDES

	Rates per thousand for children of attempted suicide	Annual rates per thousand for the city
Juvenile delinquency	113·6	24·0
Children taken into care	272·7	3·4
Persistent truancy	272·7	2·1
RSSPCC referrals	136·4	6·6

are incomplete and existing children are too young to be at risk for some variables. Truancy tends to be more common later in school life, and few of the children of our patients had attained school-leaving age. The second point concerns the accuracy with which the incidence of this variable has been recorded since the criterion for this variable was that a parent had been summoned before the Education Committee to account for absences. For the patients themselves there was always the danger that despite careful repetition of this criterion they might still give as truancy the odd day "spent fishing". However, where their own children were concerned, parents would know whether or not they had been summoned, and hence the reporting is more accurate.

These children have incomplete lifetime rates for having been taken into care and for RSSPCC referrals which are very similar to those of their parents. Viewed overall, these children show just as marked social pathology as their parents—a disturbing state of affairs which will be discussed later under prevention.

The Value of Simple Ecological Analyses

Clearly in our work in Edinburgh the value of looking at the ecological aspects of suicidal behaviour has been demonstrated. Social variables of the kind described in this chapter are useful in two ways; they act as global indices of the social condition of any city and they have value as stimulants in providing new ideas and hypotheses to explore in individuals. It was found that the collection and analysis of the data were very economical both in terms of time and money, but it is very clear that in order to use ecological data in any more detailed way it would be necessary to deal with a wide variety of methodological problems. The essential concern must be with people, and it would not be profitable to be caught up in irrelevant pursuits. In any setting, a judicious use of existing reports and annual statistical returns can highlight other associations with suicidal behaviour which have not yet come to light.

CHAPTER 5

The Concept of Suicide

ALTHOUGH at the beginning of this book we said that we did not wish to focus much attention on completed suicide, it is necessary to have some clear idea of what suicide really means before it is possible to discuss prophylaxis.

In using the term suicide we are in no way concerned with its legal definition, which seeks only to create statistics. Indeed, the legal viewpoint has done much to confuse the issue. Given that coroners are honourable and humane men, it is left to them to place each fatality into a classificatory compartment—not to try to understand why the person died. But this means that if a coroner decides to be charitable to the living when the evidence is equivocal, then what to the experienced clinician was suicide becomes misadventure or accident.

From a legal viewpoint suicide is only thought of as an act of commission, when people *do* something. This viewpoint ignores fatalities which are caused by deliberate *failure* to do something. For example, the suicidal diabetic simply fails to take insulin, and it is highly improbable that any coroner will think of such a case as suicide. Many road fatalities might, by a similar process, be considered to be accidents rather than suicides.

As we have shown in Chapter 2, there are certain necessary factors which must be present before a fatality can be called a suicide. There must be some evidence of premeditation, however short, some evidence of action so planned as to intend death and there must be access to a method of achieving this intent. Looking again at our hypothetical diabetic, we would have to demonstrate that he had thought of ending his life, that he had available supplies of insulin, and that he took the action of *not* taking insulin, which would in the absence of intervention cause his death. Reference to Fig. 2

(p. 39) shows that this person would have exhibited premeditation X, action towards death Y, and access to an effective method Z.

Hypothetical cases are all very well; they serve to give point to some of our arguments. What we shall now do is present a real case which shows all the problems relating to the accurate ascertainment of what actually happens when a person dies suddenly and inexplicably. In some ways the case is bizarre, but it serves to highlight the social, psychological, and medical issues which are present in suicidal behaviour. It also makes clear just how often cries for help fall on insensitive ears, not least our own, for this case which ended in self-destruction had passed through our hands before.

Farberow and Shneidman, in co-operation with the Los Angeles coroner, instituted a form of psycho-social investigation of all cases where suicide was suspected in that city. This investigation was modelled on the post-mortem procedures employed in physical medicine and was given the name "psychological autopsy". Briefly, this procedure involved an investigation by a psychologist or social worker who tried to reconstruct the events preceding and leading up to the suicide. They found that information of this kind was of great value to coroners whose task it was to reach a verdict.

During the course of our work in the Poisoning Treatment Centre we have known many cases where persons who have attempted suicide have, at some later date, killed themselves. The case about to be presented is unique, since not only were medical, social, and psychological data about her hospital admissions available, but she was one of the group of patients who featured in our psychological re-test study discussed in Chapter 3, and in addition the kind of psychological autopsy suggested by Farberow and Shneidman was conducted. Chapter 1 presented two cases in which the effects of childhood influences were shown to have some bearing on suicidal behaviour in adult life and in the last chapter we expanded somewhat on this theme. Chapter 3 discussed the salient personality features of attempted suicides and showed that as a group they showed marked character disorder and much emotional upset. Throughout previous chapters the dangers of relating specific social problems to suicidal behaviour in a causal way have been reiterated. These problems frequently describe the personality of the patient rather than predict any specific event. Many of these comments are exemplified by the following case.

CASE 10. *Mrs. M.*

The psychological autopsy began when we were notified that Mrs. M. had died of a massive overdose of a mixture of barbiturate drugs accompanied by alcohol. The first phase of the examination was to check back on the existing medical and social records, where a history was found which revealed the following.

Family history

Father. Information about the patient's father is somewhat scanty. He died of cancer of the stomach at the age of 52 when the patient was 8 years old. According to the social history he had never worked in his life and was entirely dependent on his wife's earnings. He was known to have drunk at least a bottle of whisky every day and since drunkenness and squabbling with his wife were synonymous the home atmosphere for the children must have been very disruptive. To add further to this disruption he was a member of the Orange Order (a militant Protestant movement), while his wife was "a good Roman Catholic". During his terminal illness he remained at home, where he died in terrible pain. The patient was the favourite of his five children.

Mother. She was still alive at the time of the patient's suicide. She was very old but in good health. During her entire life she neither drank nor smoked; she is described as being a worrier. There appears to have been no strong relationship between her and the patient, who said "that in all her life she had never confided in her about anything". This was rationalized by saying, "I hid things from her because she was a worrier."

Siblings. The first child died from an unknown cause at the age of 2 years, before the patient was born. The second child, a girl, was killed in an air raid during the war, at which time she was 18 years old. Two other siblings, both older, are somewhat vague figures, largely because the patient had long ceased to have contact with them.

Comment. Constant and satisfying relationships are important aspects for the development of a healthy personality; it can be seen from the history thus far that it is unlikely that either of these existed for Mrs. M. It is of interest that relationships with her siblings and particularly with her mother were almost non-existent.

Personal history

For most of her very early life it is necessary to guess at the depth of personal satisfaction she obtained, but we feel certain that this must have been minimal. Despite the description of her father, his death when she was aged 8, when she watched his suffering, appears to have been a traumatic experience in her life; she saw herself as his favourite. Her school life appears to have been uneventful and unspectacular. She said that she left school at the age of 14 years in order to "help the family finances", but since these finances must have improved greatly following the death of her father, the marriage of her older sister, and the move into employment of her brother, it is likely that she actually left school for more mundane reasons.

There is some evidence that her early emotional experiences may have had an adverse effect because at the age of 16 she became pregnant by a Dutch sailor. She was aware that he was an extremely heavy drinker and "an atrocious liar". He had also been treated in local mental hospitals for a paranoid illness. Nonetheless she married him, but within a year, when he was abroad, she had an affair with another man. Later in the same year her husband returned and a reconciliation was effected, but "he never forgave me". Somehow or other the marriage continued until 3 years before her death, when she left him because "life had become impossible".

She was finally divorced the year before her death. After leaving her husband she worked for a very short time and was then totally dependent on alimony from her husband and National Assistance support. This small amount of money must have made practical living difficult, since there were five children to support.

Children. The oldest child, a girl, became pregnant when aged 16. At the time of the patient's death, she and her illegitimate child lived in the maternal home together with her co-habitee. The second child, a boy, was committed to an approved school at the age of 13 and was still there when his mother died. The youngest children, a girl aged 13 and twin boys aged 9, were at local schools and so far as is known they manifested no abnormalities.

Comment. This woman has shown the unfortunate habit of moving from one crisis to another in a very insightless fashion. There is clear evidence of a shallowness in her personal relations which was further confirmed by her having confessed to never having had any close friends. The reader will have noted how a drunken father was succeeded by a drunken husband and how her own early pregnancy was followed in similar fashion by her daughter. It is seen in her comment about the break-up of her marriage—"life had become impossible"—that the first seeds of her suicidal thoughts were already present.

General background

The first known point of contact with psychiatric and social work services was some 16 months before her death, at the instigation of a general practitioner who, referring her to hospital, said, "This patient has been weepy and depressed for some months. She has been getting a lot worse." The referring letter went on to point out that there was a history of abuse of tranquillizing drugs and barbiturates which extended over a period of about 9 years, with some suggestion that these drugs were being obtained illegally. The social situation at this point was that she was in debt to the extent of £200, including arrears of rent, electricity, and gas. There must have been grave danger of eviction and break-up of the family, and this must have been particularly worrying for the patient since some 2 years previously she had been evicted for arrears of rent and for keeping an immoral house. The known social problems at that earlier time concerned drugs, drink, and men.

Comment. It is of interest that when these very severe problems came to a head 2 years earlier, referral for psychiatric investigation was met with official indifference which had a punitive flavour.

Mental state

On examination by a psychiatrist Mrs. M. was described as an anxious person and a worrier with no close friends in whom to confide. There was no evidence of organic impairment and despite the reason for her referral by the general practitioner no depressive features were elicited, and no comment was made about drugs. Comment was made about her heavy smoking and drinking. In summary, she was not seen as presenting with a psychiatric problem and the psychiatrist's general impression was "a problem reactive to her social rather than any underlying psychiatric condition".

Comment. Apart from these initial social and psychiatric investigations the patient received only the offer of an out-patient appointment which she did not keep.

The next we hear of her is 2 months later when she was admitted to hospital following an overdose of barbiturate. The consultant psychiatrist at that time made a primary diagnosis of alcoholism and it was suggested that she drank at least one bottle of vodka every day. As far as the overdose was concerned, the patient denied having had any intention of killing herself and professed a memory blackout for taking the pills at all. She did admit that earlier on the day of her admission she had had a row with her daughter in which the police were involved. She also denied being alcoholic. For the first time some evidence of epilepsy was noted, although her general practitioner, a different one this time, said he was satisfied these were of hysterical origin. She failed to keep two appointments offered to her.

Nine months later she was admitted again to hospital suffering from an overdose of barbiturates. Her family described her admission this time as being "accidental since she was no more drugged at the time of admission than she usually was, when they allowed her to sleep it off". On this occasion her daughter's co-habitee contacted the family doctor, who again referred her to hospital. During examination she admitted to two forms of enjoyment—drinking and taking barbiturates. She said there was nothing wrong with her but admitted to having some social problems which she said were insurmountable. She denied any suicidal intent and demanded to leave the ward "so that she could straighten out matters at home". Before leaving hospital she was started on phenobarbitone for her alleged epilepsy.

On this admission she was interviewed and tested by the present authors. Her psychological test results were typical of the group, in that she was character disordered and very anxious indeed.

Comment. Although on two occasions this woman had denied any suicidal thoughts, she had on both occasions displayed deliberate drug-taking behaviour. On the second occasion she actually described her situation as being "hopeless". These denials are further evidenced by her attitude towards alcohol, probably a form of escapism, and provide more evidence that she lacked insight. This lack is still further demonstrated by the fact that despite two admissions for self-poisoning within 9 months, she refused further help, although on the second occasion she did agree to have a social worker call for a "check up" a month after discharge.

Soon afterwards she was admitted again to hospital having taken barbiturates with alcohol and having been involved in a drunken brawl. Again she denied addiction to either drugs or alcohol, but the psychiatric registrar was of the opinion that "she did not want help and it is doubtful whether help can be given to her. She is presently quite happy with the way her life is progressing."

She reappeared in hospital after another brief interval, having taken a similar mixture of drugs and alcohol, but was discharged with a slightly different treatment regime. This time she was invited to contact the hospital when she felt in need of help rather than resoit to another overdose. This admission was followed almost immediately by her being brought once again to hospital by the police in a drunken state and claiming to have taken an overdose of barbiturates. Examination showed traces of drugs which could be accounted for by her anticonvulsant treatment, and on discharge she was again exhorted to contact the ward when she needed help.

Comment. It is apparent that this patient made repeated cries for help which were being monitored but not heard. It is interesting to note that on her last admission she claimed to have taken an overdose, and here perhaps was a final plea to be heard. This, coming from a person who had repeatedly used denial in her relationship with psychiatrists, was perhaps a significant change.

During the ensuing days Mrs. M. called at her general practitioner. It is not clear what the aim of this visit was, but probably it was some attempt to obtain drugs. He referred her to a psychiatric clinic with the expressed hope that she would be seen as an emergency. Having presented herself with the doctor's letter at the clinic she was told that she could not be seen until 2 days later. This time she remembered the invitation to use the resources of the General Hospital and, without

D

having taken any overdose, sought help there. This help took the form of enabling her to be seen by a senior psychiatrist that day, but nothing positive arose from this consultation.

During the days that followed she recovered her spirits and completed and posted to us the psychological re-test questionnaires discussed in Chapter 3, but on the day these reached us we heard of her death. These test results showed no change from the picture she presented at the first time of testing.

Psycho-social autopsy

The first step was to contact this patient's general practitioner, and it transpired that she had called on him on the day following her last contact with the psychiatrist, saying that she was unwell and required sedation. According to the doctor she appeared to be bright, cheery, calm, and undrugged, and he refused to give her a prescription. Apparently about a month earlier the patient's mother had contacted him to say that she was over-indulging in drugs, and this is consistent with her movements over that period. It must be remembered that she changed general practitioners very frequently, and it is not surprising that this one had to be told about her drug abuse. We were also informed that the barbiturates which had been in part responsible for her death had been prescribed by yet another doctor. It also transpired that other supplies of barbiturates had been purchased illegally by her.

Following one of her admissions to hospital several months earlier, the patient had agreed to have a social worker visit her but this was never effected. At a further admission it was arranged that another social worker would call and this in fact was carried out. When the social worker arrived at the patient's house she found Mrs. M. lying on the floor under the influence of drink and probably drugs also. An attempt was made to have her seen at the local psychiatric out-patient clinic, but unfortunately some time passed between the instigation of this visit and the appointment given her, and by this time she had taken another overdose and was admitted to hospital.

The next step in the psychological autopsy was to contact the police, the main aim being to find out when the patient's funeral was to take place so that the relatives could be contacted at the least painful moment.

It was also hoped that they would provide further information, but in the event they did not.

The adult members of the family were then interviewed. All of them were very willing to talk—indeed, grateful for the opportunity. They appeared almost relieved about the patient's death and all showed a great deal of anger at the facility with which she had been able to get drugs. Mrs. M. apparently died in the house of a woman who in the past had frequently supplied her with drugs and who was also in the habit of exchanging drugs for whisky in a local tavern.

On the evening following her last visit to her general practitioner Mrs. M. had a seizure, but whether this was due to epilepsy or drug withdrawal cannot be said. On the day following she managed to get a prescription for drugs from another doctor, but during that day she had neither the appearance of being drugged nor had she been drinking. This was unusual. The following morning she left to go shopping and was returned to the house in the middle of the day by a passing motorist who had found her staggering in a helpless condition in the street. Her daughter said that this was due to drug abuse rather than drink. She recovered quickly and by evening appeared to be her normal self. At about 6 p.m. she went out with the woman known to be a "pusher" and all that the family knew of the events which followed was that a great deal of alcohol had been drunk by the patient, her woman friend, and two men who were also known to over-indulge in drink and drugs. After bar closing time they repaired to the pusher's home and presumably continued their revelry. In the early hours of the morning knocking at the door of the flat aroused the man on whose knee Mrs. M. had fallen asleep. He rose to answer the caller, and on his return to share the chair thought that she was rather cold—she was in fact dead and the police were called.

The family also divulged that in addition to the times Mrs. M. had been admitted to hospital there had been many occasions when drugs had produced unconsciousness. On one occasion they had allowed her to sleep for 48 hours, assuming that she had taken only a few tablets. Only after this did they attempt to estimate how many tablets had been taken. It was found that indeed she had taken a large overdose and our informant told us "she could easily have been dead that time".

An attempt was made to contact the pusher, but on both occasions we called she was so intoxicated as to be incapable of giving any information.

This case is presented in full detail in the hope that the reader will be able to relate to it the more hypothetical case illustrations given earlier in the book. It is presented also because it highlights the findings of our more formal research. This case shows probable evidence of the importance of early, satisfying, warm interpersonal relations in the development of personality. It also shows how personal disorganization can be repeated through the generations. The case also highlights the social disorganization and poor living conditions described in Chapter 4. Where there is a chronic lack of money there is a constant threat to the continuity of cohesive family life and the gross responses to this kind of threat.

An interesting feature of this case was the patient's apparent inability to make relationships, even with persons skilled in the art. This is best illustrated by her repeated use of denial as a means of rationalizing her overdoses. A problem for anyone working with such patients is that of evaluating both verbal and non-verbal behaviour, and therefore knowing when therapeutically useful changes present. All too often a diagnostic label, however well formulated, tends to crystallize attitudes and make changes in treatment more difficult to envisage.

Had Mrs. M. died in England there is little doubt that a coroner would have been led by the evidence to return a verdict of death by misadventure. Yet there is no doubt that this woman, in a sense, died by her own hand. As will be seen in the next chapter, people who repeatedly take overdoses of drugs can be typified by this case. There is little doubt that the chronic self-poisoner carries a very poor prognosis as regards living. Clearly prevention in this kind of case must be aimed at preventing chronicity.

CHAPTER 6

Sequelae of Suicidal Behaviour

A Follow-up Study of Attempted Suicides

It is shown that distress, despair and unhappiness, poor interpersonal relationships, social disorganization, and adverse early experiences are all notable features of attempted suicide. With the enormous increase in this kind of behaviour over the past decade there must be not only an increase in the facilities provided for treatment but also the most appropriate treatment for each case must be provided. Deciding on this for each patient is a difficult task unless one is equipped with some knowledge as to how patients who have attempted suicide have progressed in the months following their admission to hospital and to learn more about the factors which relate to good or bad social prognoses. It was inevitable that one of the serial studies mentioned in Chapter 2 which was conducted by the Edinburgh researchers should make some effort to add to this gap in knowledge, and to this end 511 patients who had been admitted to hospital following a suicidal attempt were re-assessed 4 months and 12 months after their discharge from the Poisoning Treatment Centre. Information was gathered systematically during these follow-up visits so that it was comparable with data collected at the time of the patient's admission to hospital. While patients were being treated physically after the event a full social history was collected from a key informant, and this was amalgamated with the patient's own story after physical recovery. After each follow-up visit, assessment of social change was made under three categories. A grading of *better* was made when the scale formed by the precipitating factors in the suicidal attempt showed amelioration and where any new factors present were not seen by the patient to be having as adverse an effect on their daily life as those factors which were present at the time of admission. A grading of *same* or *no change* was made where there was no

89

change in those items listed as precipitating factors at the time of admission
or where, if there was change for the better in any such items, new ones,
seen by the patient as being equally severe, had replaced them. A grading of
worse was made where there was deterioration in any of the items listed as
precipitating factors at the time of admission or, although there was no
change in these items, new and equally severe problems had presented.
These gradings were made following an interview with the patient,
together with the information gathered from key informants and from the
patient's own assessment of change. It is of interest that *all* the patients
admitted to the Poisoning Treatment Centre during the course of a year
agreed to participate in the investigation and that the follow-up yielded a
98·6 per cent response after four months and 99·6 per cent after a year.
There was no antagonism to the follow-up visits, and it is believed that
this was because this group of patients felt that at a time when they felt
helpless and hopeless they *did* have something to contribute which might
be helpful to others in similar distressful situations in the future. Perhaps
another factor in the success of these follow-up visits was that the inter-
viewer was known to all the patients because of his contact with them as a
member of the "team" who ministered to them during the crisis situation.

The periods for the follow-up visits were chosen because it was felt that
at 4 months changes in the behaviour of the patient, spouse, kin, and friends
might still be related to the attempted suicide but not too greatly influenced
by its immediate impact, while at 12 months sufficient time would have
elapsed for new problems to have arisen and therefore for temporary
effects of the act to be observed by comparing the data gathered at the
second follow-up visit with those gathered at the first. Only 26 men and
47 women so followed-up showed differences in their social state between
the two visits, and so the observed results after 4 months can largely be
extended to the 12-month assessment.

The Edinburgh researches are used extensively to support our comment,
but the reader is cautioned that while generalizations can be made with
reasonably complete accuracy for a whole group, the implications of such
generalizations can in no sense be used to predict the behaviour of any
individual within the group or even within any of the identifiable subgroups.

For clarity of presentation there will be separate discussions on the social
factors which appear to be associated with changes in social functioning

found in the group as a whole and the factors which differentiate those who have repeated episodes of suicidal behaviour, some of which prove to be fatal.

Changes in functioning were assessed in three areas:

1. *The demographic area.* This included the variables of age; marital state; social class; work record; place and type of residence; and usual living arrangements.
2. *The clinical area.* In this area the variables studied included the relationship which the patient had with the key person in the event; the method used in the suicidal attempt; the assessed motive for the attempt; the degree of life endangerment involved; the patient's mental state at the time of the event; and the presence of any character disorder.
3. *Precipitating factors.* This area was concerned with kin disharmony; work problems; problems of unemployment or pending unemployment; financial problems; bereavement; crime; gambling; alcohol; problems of housing; and problems concerned with sex.

Each of these areas was investigated to see whether or not they related to subsequent change in the patients' social state or in their or the key person's behaviour.

Factors Associated with Social Prognosis

DEMOGRAPHIC VARIABLES

Age. For both sexes there was found to be a very strong tendency for people under the age of 35 years to show more social improvement than people in older age groups.

Marital state. Investigation of this variable revealed that the social state of patients whose marriages were still functioning improved more often and deteriorated less often than any of the other categories.

Social class. For men, social class appears to have no bearing on subsequent social functioning, but it does appear to be an important factor for women. It was found that women in social class III showed improvement in their social state more than women in the other social classes. Social classes I, II, and III were similar in the amount to social deterioration, and they showed only half the amount of deterioration manifested by the lower classes.

*Work record.** It was not surprising to find that men whose work record had been categorized as *fair* improved in their social state more often than those with *better* or *worse* work records. Since work and social functioning are very closely related, those with only *fair* records had more scope for change than those with better records and, by definition, were not so hopeless as those with bad records.

Residence. Patients who lived in dwellings other than in homes either owned or rented by them exclusively showed deterioration in their social state much more often than those who lived in their own homes.

Living arrangements. So far as men were concerned, those whose marriage had broken for any reason and who lived alone formed the most static group so far as social state after a suicide attempt was concerned. The group of patients who lived with parents or with friends or relatives showed much more change in either direction, but showed improvement almost twice as frequently as men who lived alone.

For women, living arrangements appeared to have little influence on changes in social state although there was a slight tendency for women who lived with their parents to show improvement more frequently than other women.

CLINICAL VARIABLES

Only two of these variables, *relationship with the key person* and *life endangerment*, were unrelated to subsequent social change.

Method. Patients who used any method other than the ingestion of drugs or the inhalation of household gas in their attempt tended to deteriorate

---

* Work record criteria. *Excellent* = fully employed with regular promotion or holding a position of responsibility over a prolonged period and where any changes in employment have been in the nature of promotion or self-betterment. *Good* = fully employed during all of adult life with or without job changes but where status tends to be static. *Fair* = employment which falls below potential capability with or without occasional periods of unemployment not exceeding 3 months in any year. *Poor* = frequent periods of unemployment with frequent job changes due mainly to industrial or other misconduct, unexplained absences, or prolonged ill health. Work of a non-steady nature. *Bad* = prolonged unemployment for any reason or erratic employment unrelated to capability or work availability.

socially after the act much more than those who used these more conventional meth*o*ds, while patients who had taken overdoses of salicylates tended to improve socially more often than those who used any other method.

Motive. Motive for the attempt in this series of studies was assessed by the clinical team of psychiatrists and social workers and was based on information supplied by the patient and by key informants. Where the clinical team felt that the motive for the act was basically concerned with fractures in personal relationships it was found that this group of patients showed more frequent change in their social state at follow-up than the group whose motive was more concerned with material circumstances or other factors and, generally speaking, these changes were for the better.

Mental state. Not surprisingly, the social functioning of patients of both sexes whose mental state changed in the interval between the act and reassessment ameliorated almost twice as frequently as that of patients whose mental state remained unchanged.

PRECIPITATING FACTORS

Of the factors which were considered to have precipitated the suicide attempts, only two yielded any significant association with subsequent change in social state, one of these being significant for men and the other significant for women. Work problems, problems of unemployment or pending unemployment, financial problems, bereavement, crime, alcohol, housing problems, and sex problems—which were frequently associated with attempted suicide—had no apparent relationship with subsequent social adjustment. Of the two precipitating factors which had associations, one showed that where women had attempted suicide in relation to kin disharmony they improved socially much more frequently than women who did not have such disturbed relationships as precipitants. The only other significant factor and which concerned men only was concerned with gambling, and when this was given as a precipitating factor social deterioration occurred twice as frequently as in cases where gambling was not a feature.

Changes in behaviour. At follow-up, it was found that when patients had changed their own behaviour for the better in relation to their pre-attempt behaviour, when they appeared to be more settled, contented, and better

E

able to cope with everyday things, their social state improved more often and deteriorated less often than was the case for patients whose behaviour remained the same. This was particularly the case when the suicidal attempt was seen to have been precipitated in some way by their previous actions.

Another less striking finding was that when a key person's behaviour regarding infidelity, pathological jealousy, drinking, gambling, or getting into debt altered for the better, then the social state of the patient improved twice as often and deteriorated less often than in cases where the key person's behaviour did not improve.

In terms of treatment and of secondary prevention it is essential that useful prognostic indicators are found. Our findings certainly suggest that social data add greatly to this task and, indeed, are likely to play a more important part than clinical data. So far as the clinical variables listed on page 92 were concerned, some had a bearing on social change but others did not. From the prognostic point of view, the person who cuts himself or who makes his attempt in one of the more "active" ways like strangulation or suffocation is likely to fare badly in the months following the attempt, while people who take overdoses of salicylates tend to do well socially.

A great deal has been written about the manipulative aim of some suicidal attempts, and we have certainly been able to demonstrate that when an attempt has been made in order to effect a modification in a relationship it does produce a change in social state subsequently. We have found that although changes in the key person's behaviour were related to changes in the patient's social state, changes in the patient's own behaviour played a much more crucial part in the social outcome of the act.

Improvement in behaviour was commonly found to be associated with changes in attitude towards key people, and a seemingly new-found ability to discuss problems with them in an atmosphere which was calmer and more constructive than before. It is suggested that a partial explanation for this change is to be found in the fact that key persons were involved immediately in the treatment situation during the crisis period so that "old ways" got less chance to become re-established when the patients were discharged from hospital. Deterioration, on the other hand—certainly in so far as marriages are concerned—appears to be more associated with changes for the worse in the spouses' behaviour. Certainly, there is little doubt that successful manipulation takes place when the patient, rather than the key person, changes his behaviour, and these changes are probably the result of the patient's reappraisal of himself and of his interpersonal relationships. Sometimes, of course, fractures in interpersonal relationships are caused by mental illness, and so it is not surprising that changes in mental health are associated more frequently with changes for the better in social functioning than with deterioration. Patients who are not mentally ill when they behave in a suicidal manner tend to have more extreme social problems, so that for them it is equally not surprising that a worsening or static social state would be more likely to result. So far as precipitating factors are concerned there are complications in their use as prognostic indicators.

Financial problems, alcohol, crime, and many of the other precipitants listed on page 93, which are associated with attempted suicide, are usually of long standing and they rarely present singly. As precipitants they contribute very little to the prediction of a patient's social prognosis, but as long-standing features of his total life situation some of them at least are predictive of future behaviour.

Factors such as crime, alcoholism, and gambling are frequently also associated with defects in personality, and the chronic inability of such individuals to maintain any improvement in their behaviour is reflected in the fact that of the seventy-three patients referred to earlier who deteriorated socially between the 4-month and the 12-month assessments, over half were character disordered.

Factors Associated with Repeated Attempts at Suicide

When a person makes a further attempt at suicide it must be assumed that his social state is worse or no better than it was on his first admission to hospital, and it is important for many reasons to study the features of people who have multiple attempts. This is especially so since upwards of one-sixth of persons first admitted to hospital following a suicidal attempt are likely to repeat their act *within the course of a single year* and one-quarter of them will repeat within 3 years unless new treatment regimes which are more successful than the present ones can be found. In addition, 3–5 per cent of them will kill themselves.

What are the characteristics of this group of people and can anything be done to help to reduce its number? There have been many studies throughout the world which have sought to identify the characteristics of the repeat-prone attempted suicide, and generally they are agreed about some of the demographic and clinical features of this group.

The majority of people who attempt suicide are under 40 years old, but when one compares groups of repeaters with first attempters there is a clear indication that the former group tend to be a little older than the latter since they are over-represented in the age group 25–35 years and under-represented in the younger groups.

Marriages which are continuing appear to be a protecting influence since people who repeat are more often either single or those whose marriages have ended by divorce or separation. As we have discussed earlier, difficulty in interpersonal relationships is an important precipitating factor, and so it is not surprising that failure with the type of close relationship necessary for a satisfactory marriage should also be an indication of repeated attempted suicide.

Generally speaking, psychotropic drugs and hypnotics are the most common agents of acts of attempted suicide, and there is little difference to be found between people who repeat the act and those who do not. There is no particular poison associated with repetition, but there is a slight tendency for those who injure themselves, generally by cutting, to repeat the act more often than those who use other methods.

There have been many attempts to classify the potential severity of attempted suicides, none of which are completely satisfactory. Whatever the method of classification, there does not appear to be any relationship between the initial classification and subsequent repetition. In the Edinburgh studies a scale was devised to categorize endangerment to life, viz. *death, death probable, death unlikely,* and *certain to survive,* but, like other researchers, we were forced to deduce that no prediction could be made from an examination of the so-called "seriousness" of what the patient did since the repeat acts were sometimes more life endangering than the initial episode, sometimes less so, and sometimes equally so.

Compared with non-repeaters, those who repeat their suicidal behaviour are mainly to be found among those patients given a primary or secondary diagnosis of pathological personality, most being sociopaths. While one-half of first attempters have normal personalities, only one-fifth of repeaters can be so considered. The part played by alcoholism in repeated attempted suicide cannot be over-emphasized since almost one-half of repeaters are alcoholics or problem drinkers. This compares with only one-fifth of first attempters. In the suicidal attempt itself it has been found that repeaters are much more often under the influence of alcohol than are first attempters. Like alcohol, drug-dependency is a more serious problem in repeaters, being twice as common in this group.

A history of psychiatric treatment prior to or at the time of the first attempt is highly associated with repetition. This is a very startling finding when one considers that almost two-thirds of repeaters have a history of psychiatric treatment compared with one-fifth of first attempters.

A feature of those who repeatedly present with suicidal behaviour is the multiplicity of their social malaise. More than one-third of this group are likely to be unemployed compared with only one-fifth of people who have not had a previous attempt. In the years preceding their admission they tend to change jobs more frequently than the other group. Almost twice as many repeaters as non-repeaters tend to live in non-family situations and in conditions of serious overcrowding, more than a third of them at the time of repetition living in lodgings, hostels, and other institutions. There is a tendency for both attempted suicide and completed suicide to be more common in the families of repeaters, these families also having higher rates of psychiatric treatment than first attempters. Debt, imprisonment, and criminal convictions are all features which are much more common in people who repeat than in the general population of suicide attempters. It has been suggested by many writers that those who act impulsively do so because they are frustrated. In addition to this it is likely that impulsive, tension-relieving behaviour can also result from acute distress. Some patients are prone to become distressed to a degree which they cannot tolerate, often when they are drunk. Whether distress is a feature of a depressive illness or of intolerable social circumstances, it is almost always present when a person attempts to take his life. Suddenly the situation becomes unbearable and something has to be done to relieve the situation, often without thought to the outcome. To the outsider there may be no obvious motive to the act. Although the majority of people who repeatedly attempt suicide do so for reasons such as these, there is a small group whose behaviour requires a different explanation. Sometimes a clinical failure to recognize or adequately treat a depression results in a further act of self-poisoning. Sometimes the short-term success of the appeal which underlay the first act prompts a further attempt. However, most of this minority group probably repeat the act because the initial act failed to bring relief.

In conclusion, people who repeatedly make attempts at suicide differ from other attempted suicides along the same dimensions as attempted suicides as a whole differ from normals. In their psychiatric features, personality characteristics and level of social functioning people who repeat are the most deviant of all.

Among those who repeat their suicidal behaviour there are those who die. In general this group tends to have in excess alcoholism, drug dependence, and all those other variables which mark out the repeater. Perhaps the most outstanding feature which separates this group from the main population of attempted suicides is that they almost always have a history of previous attempts. However, we would remind the reader that while one-quarter of completed suicides have had a known history of prior attempts, the majority would seem to succeed at their first attempt.

CHAPTER 7

Implications for Prevention

PREVENTION of suicidal behaviour can be considered under the three customary headings—primary, secondary, and tertiary. *Primary* prevention is concerned with efforts aimed at preventing the existence of suicidal behaviour in any form; *secondary* prevention has as its aim the elimination of recurrent or repeated acts of self-poisoning; while *tertiary* prevention, in respect to suicidal behaviour, aims to prevent acts from having fatal outcomes. In considering primary and secondary prevention it is imperative to gain insight into suicidal behaviour, and for this reason it is conventional to discuss these several aspects of prevention in reverse order.

Tertiary

So far as *tertiary* prevention is concerned, this is a matter for toxicologists and physicians, and is, hence, outside the scope of this book. In passing, however, it is clear that improved medical techniques, such as renal dialysis, have resuscitated patients who in years past would have died. Thus an improvement in tertiary prevention has resulted in a blurring of what was once thought to be a clear-cut boundary between suicide and attempted suicide. Unfortunately, too many teachers cling to the notion that to be unsuccessful in a suicidal attempt is to have "failed", and that such failure is strong evidence of a poor personality. They use the age-old erroneous argument that an unsuccessful suicidal attempt demonstrates that the attempter can do nothing well—including bringing about his own demise. This is an extremely distorted and harmful point of view. For many reasons, persons who are truly intent on dying may live after a suicidal attempt. These reasons include unexpected or chance intervention from the environment (the Z factor), lack of sophisticated pharmacological knowledge, and improvements in medical treatment. This latter reason in particular means that many people who, but for skilled therapy, would have died and been classed as (successful) suicide must now be classed as attempted suicide. Changes such as these make a mockery of attempts to classify suicidal behaviour into neat categories.

Secondary

In general terms secondary prevention is concerned with individuals who have identified themselves by a suicidal act and from the study of these individuals we can glean information which may, in the first instance, help us prevent further incidents on their part. As part of our series of studies we have attempted to relate information gathered about patients at the time of their admission to further self-poisoning acts. In this way it is possible to identify the salient features of people who run a high risk of repeating their suicidal behaviour—sometimes with fatal results. The first three chapters have described the social, psychiatric, and psychological characteristics which are available for use in identifying potential repeaters. Regardless of fluctuations in admission rates, the proportion of patients admitted who are repeaters remains constant, a feature which has facilitated the construction of prediction scales. At the time of writing these scales seem to be more useful in predicting further suicidal behaviour in women than in men. From complex scales taking into account social and psychiatric factors it proved possible to form low-, medium-, and high-risk groups for men and women. It was found on follow-up that the probability of repeating for men was 13 per cent in the low-risk group, 32 per cent in the medium, and 57 per cent in the high-risk category. For women the probabilities were 8, 31, and 56 per cent respectively.

Primary

In the wider sense this information may be used to help in the identification of groups of people in the community who, while not having attempted suicide, may be at risk. Such identification is the first step towards primary prevention, which is the most difficult to achieve of the three goals. Chapter 4 pointed out the important role played by ecological research in spelling out the characteristics of communities.

Active Intervention—The Matching of Patient and Therapist

The authors have tried to show throughout this book that the personality characteristics and social features of people who behave in a suicidal fashion complement one another and are inextricably intertwined. The "behaviour" of these people is a process viewed from two different professional standpoints. A cardinal feature of this process, seen from both vantage points, is a striking inability to maintain satisfying interpersonal relationships. An attempt is now made to examine some of the wider implications of this inability from each professional viewpoint before attempting a synthesis which precedes thoughts about preventative measures.

Interpersonal relationships, however viewed, are a crucial feature of human existence, and the person who cannot maintain such relationships lacks integration as a person and, indeed, has little satisfaction from life. Before one can consider prevention in the primary and secondary stages it is necessary to have some conception of the integrated individual and the aims of integration. These have been so well described by Foulds (1965) in the following passage:

". . . the integrative individual, knowing who he is, can risk allowing himself to become vulnerable and thus to become capable of entering into a mutual relationship. The partially integrated individual, fearing the possibility of modification, of rejection, of further disintegration, cannot allow himself to become vulnerable and thus cannot enter into mutual personal relationships. By protecting himself, by his inability to reveal himself, he precludes the possibility of knowing himself, and, more particularly, of knowing others.

"A mutual personal relationship exists when both individuals are capable predominantly of intending their own actions (which implies that any unconscious motivation will not be such as seriously to disrupt such intentions); when both individuals predominantly succeed in communicating both cognitively and affectively to a sufficient, but not necessarily conscious, degree to make possible a sharing of experience; when each individual acts predominantly for the sake of the other. It is not merely that the members of the orchestra comprehend the gestures of the conductor and that the conductor hears and appreciates the tonal values and the tempo of their mutual production. Out of the music written down by the composer, out of the imagined interpretation of the conductor, out of his and the orchestra's execution emerges a unique performance of the work. The musical notation represents those dominant traits and attitudes that are awakened by personal interacting, the issue of which may transcend the previous expectations of each. Once having thus been elicited these emergent qualities are added to the reservoir of potentialities for the future."

The partially or poorly integrated individual can be typified by any of our patients, but especially by an individual such as Mrs. M. (p. 81). We can see in her case how defences, prominently of denial, were used to prevent adequate mutuality and to mask the cry for help. Where two people are involved in a transaction of a therapeutic nature there can be little satisfaction for either until there is a real two-way relationship. Like the orchestra, the product of such a relationship is greater than the sum of each individual's investment. We know that there is no satisfaction for a therapist in a treatment situation where the chances of failure are high. Equally we know that by his attempts to escape from a life situation of hopelessness, and by his inability to express such hopelessness in behaviour which is less hazardous than self-poisoning, there can be no satisfaction for the patient. Whatever else therapy might entail, it must include steps taken by the therapist to make himself accessible to the patient's communications, however expressed, at a level which must be determined by the patient. This is simply because, being more integrated, the therapist must be better able to accept modification or, as in the case of Mrs. M., rejection.

Chapter 6 showed that the most striking improvement found in the social state of patients who had attempted suicide occurred in those cases where modifications in the behaviour of the chief protagonists resulted. This was most striking where the attempter was able to become "vulnerable" by expressing his true feelings, receive no rejection, and hence, having experienced a satisfying relationship, felt able to continue with a now more contented life. People who did this did not repeat their suicidal behaviour. Clearly, satisfying interpersonal relationships provide potent support when stressful situations are encountered.

It has been shown that many of our patients have suffered from early deprivation of one form or another, and the evidence suggests that this produces aberrations of personality in later life. The average person is able to cope with most of life's happenings—just how he copes depends on his particular personality make-up. A person whose essential self or ego has developed to a better-than-average degree will, using Foulds's terminology, find it easy to enter into mutual personal relationships. In the event of adversity he would be able to utilize his own resources and also those of other people; having been able to relate to them he finds no threat in asking for help. The individual with less-than-average "self-development" cannot enter easily into mutual personal relationships and so when things go wrong he has to stand alone with his scanty resources. Unfortunately, in such individuals the "cry for help" often appears to others as a cry of "wolf, wolf!". It is suggested that failure to develop a well-integrated personality is reflected in an inability to relate to other people in a mutually satisfying manner. Viewed from a social standpoint this failure appears in the form of poor mutual relationships, separation, and divorce. It is also easy to understand why a person who is not well integrated is frequently unemployed and lives in the poor housing conditions discussed in Chapter 4. It has also been shown that many supposed precipitants are in fact the projection of the patient's personality onto the social sphere and have been present for a long time. It has been our experience that a study of "precipitating factors" in suicidal behaviour frequently gives better insight into the personality and social circumstances of the patient than into the event itself.

Our suicide population is clearly one which is characterized by poor early personality development and a subsequent inability to cope with life in an effective, satisfying way. Socially this life, such as it is, is lived in conditions of physical disorganization and poor material circumstances. This formulation applies most readily to the repeat prone, the target of secondary prevention, the group of people for whom we appear to do least.

People who poison or injure themselves are generally brought to hospital; there the physician or surgeon is involved with physical recovery, the tertiary stage of prevention. For secondary prevention the usual procedure begins with the physician's call for psychiatric help. Kessel, a noted psychiatrist in this field, has suggested some of the steps that should be taken to prevent repetition. He suggests that drugs should not be prescribed for people who poison themselves unless it is certain that they cannot get at the supply, and he exhorts that this restriction should apply to the tablets of other members of the household. The general practitioner should endeavour to see that there are *no* drugs, other than those in current use, in the home of the attempter because of the impulsive nature of many suicidal attempts. If there are no pills at hand it is likely that the impulse to take them will pass. Our researches support the logic of this reasoning since we have found by investigation that patients generally remain constant to one mode of attempt and are unlikely to resort to more drastic measures.

Kessel stated categorically that many of the problems presented by the high-risk group should be handled by social work intervention. He recognized, as do the authors, the need for prolonged contact with patients. An effort to implement some of Kessel's suggestions has been made by offering psycho-social support over a period of 6 months. The psychiatrist and social worker operating this scheme concluded that this did not prevent further suicide attempts amongst this high-risk group of patients. They speculated that, since there was some apparent amelioration of the very stressful social circumstances, a larger period of contact, the prolonged period suggested by Kessel, might reduce the number of further suicidal attempts. They also acknowledged a degree of optimism in their aims of changing in so brief a time the habits and modes of dealing with stress adopted over so many years by their patients.

Earlier it was outlined how vulnerable and inadequate these patients are in their interpersonal relationships and indicated that the more integrated therapist must adjust his level of therapy to the patient's ability to absorb and interact with it. Once this is achieved we believe there is some foundation for further growth.

Perhaps the conventional psychiatric social work approach becomes the more difficult since, even though it may cover a wide span in time, conventionally it is transient by nature. That is to say, patients are given regular appointments either at a clinic or in their homes at regular intervals which rarely exceed once per week and for periods which rarely exceed an hour in duration.

Earlier in this chapter and elsewhere the need for sustained, meaningful, and satisfying relationships for this group of patients is described, and our studies have shown that, given this, the risk of repetition is reduced. If the aim in secondary prevention is to prevent further suicidal attempts among, in the main, a group of people whose *ego* or *essential self* is relatively undeveloped, then conventional psycho-social intervention is unlikely to be sufficiently successful in the short term. This high-risk group of patients are characterized by their lack of close interpersonal relationships in their everyday life, and it follows that if the therapeutic approach succeeds in making them *vulnerable* it must also be *sustained* if the patient, lacking in other satisfying relationships, is not to be overwhelmed by his new-found vulnerability. To be *vulnerable* in the Foulds sense and to live in the milieu described must indeed be dangerous for this group of people whose ego can only be, after formal psycho-social intervention over a short period, relatively undeveloped. They have few people around them to whom they can turn in the event of adversity, and may even feel rejected when they feel alone. The case of Mrs. M. (p. 81) surely typifies this—when she wanted and needed help *it was when she wanted it*, and the psychiatrist or social worker was not always available. It may well be that to say "we are here if needed" is insufficient, and that the service to this suicide-prone group must break from the conventional one and reach a hand out to them rather than to have it the other way round. The "cry for help" is frequently unheard and as frequently or even more frequently misdirected. The person who desperately feels that life is not worth living must have easy access to sympathetic ears if he is to live, and we cannot over-emphasize that no matter how trivial the crisis appears to the observer, it is often a matter of "life or death" to the patient.

Such a programme would require the careful matching of therapist and type of therapy with patient. Continuous assessment of the levels of interaction would also be necessary since changes would have to be made from time to time.

Clearly this basic plan of therapy could be elaborated in a very large number of ways, and a programme of evaluation would be needed to assess the efficacy of the various methods used. To achieve satisfactory mutual relationships of the kind set out by Foulds, this programme would require better matching of therapist, treatment model, and patient. Undoubtedly this would be a lengthy, time-consuming procedure which would be fraught with failures. To cope with such failures it would be necessary to follow Kessel's recommendation of affording emergency relief by providing a refuge where a distressed person can obtain help *when he needs it*, without having to pay the price of attempting suicide. We have seen that even a person so psychologically unstable as Mrs. M. was capable of utilizing such a refuge. Such treatment is of a different order to our somewhat idealistic long-term proposal; it is concrete, easily provided, inexpensive, very practicable and, provided it is very sincere, it can work.

These proposals for prevention may be considered to be very expensive to implement; but as demonstrated on page 15 in the case of the White family it would have been cheaper to have provided long-term support than to have allowed matters to take the course they did—to say nothing of the greater satisfaction with life that may have occurred. Even in crude economic terms our scheme is viable. Shortage of funds is not a justifiable excuse when one considers the vast sums spent "patching", while at the same time ignoring the family situation which is calculated to create a new generation of people who attempt suicide as well as producing other manifestations of deviant behaviour. Over the past decade the rates for attempted suicide have increased tenfold and, as far as the authors are aware, no satisfactory answer for this has emerged. But, if our dynamic theory is correct, each generation of attempted suicides is likely to produce proportionately more potential attempted suicides in the following generation. By dint of their relatively unsatisfactory emotional experience, many of these patients marry impulsively at an early age, have children early, and therefore experience financial hardship earlier. All these factors combine to produce a chronic stress level which is intolerable to them. The currently fashionable, and for some the "learned", way of coping is to take an overdose of drugs. In clinical practice another trend has been noted, involving the same kind of people, where drugs are taken to produce pleasure rather than to avoid pain or distress. These persons have no suicidal intent, although some may well die of a drug overdose. Whether taken for pleasure or to avoid pain, there is a large element of escapism in drug taking of this sort.

If the incidence of this form of escapism increases, then there will have to be massive rethinking about what constitutes "attempted suicide". Consider a person who takes an overdose of drugs "for kicks", misjudges the dose, and is taken to a poisoning treatment centre where he may live or die. In Chapter 2 prominence was given to *premeditation* as a major area to be investigated in understanding suicidal behaviour. To ascertain premeditation is to investigate intention and *motive*, to ask *what* a person was trying to do as well as *why* he was doing it. Our hypothetical patient's motive in taking drugs is clearly not suicidal unless we hypothesize some unconscious factor, but his behaviour can be encompassed and understood in terms of our model.

Whether a person's motive for taking drugs was to commit suicide, to escape from distress, or to gain pleasurable experience, if he takes an overdose and is admitted to hospital he must be treated. As far as tertiary prevention is concerned motive is of no consequence; the physician's task is to facilitate recovery. Secondary prevention, concerned with the modification of the patient's behaviour or that of his environment, should be concerned with motive, and this must be carefully investigated since it plays such an important part in the determination of treatment. So far as primary prevention is concerned, individual motives are of less importance. The main role of primary prevention is to deal with large-scale social re-education and prophylaxis. Of course, there are situations where individual motives are important. In a treatment situation a patient may reveal suicidal ruminations and the therapist takes steps to prevent any suicidal attempt. But, in general, primary prevention is group, rather than individual, oriented. We have postulated that suicidal behaviour, to which we must now add drug taking for kicks, is not something in which the average person indulges; it is peculiar to three recognizable groups of people.

The first of these groups comprises those who are not mentally ill and are not bowed down by stress. Their suicidal behaviour can be seen as a rational act following careful assessment of the pros and cons of living and dying. Another group behaves in a suicidal way because they are mentally ill, and we have shown that when individuals of this sort are successfully treated they may never again behave in this way. Classically, these people suffer from depression, schizophrenia, and epilepsy, and as such are the responsibility of psychiatrists, and primary prevention is most likely to lie largely in the hands of biochemists and geneticists.

The third group, which consists of people who may take drugs to seek relief or escape from stress, are characterized by psycho-social difficulties evidenced by poor interpersonal relationships and generally poor material circumstances. As we have pointed out, treatment for this group at the secondary level is extremely time-consuming and difficult. At a primary level of prevention, however, there is some hope. These people, by their way of life, are chronically at odds with the rest of society. Frequently, their housing conditions and living arrangements leave much to be desired, while the available educational facilities are often below the standards to be found in more affluent areas. Also the areas in which these people live are sadly lacking in even the most rudimentary civic amenities. Such as exist they often abuse, and this in turn lessens the likelihood of even adequate replacement. This is the kind of situation that breeds hostility. Such hostility creates prejudice so that all people living in an area become characterized by a few. And so the circle goes on.

Both collectively and individually these people have been rejected and, in turn, have rejected society. Society is too rigid and inflexible at the present time to deal with these people. How is this situation to be changed? In practice there are at least two levels of primary prevention—social crises can be combated before they develop too far and crises can be prevented from occurring. This latter can be done also at two levels: the first of these concerns the mobilization of the adult community in activities which give them hope for the future well-being of their area; the second concerns an attack on the bad parent–child relationships seen to be so prevalent in our patients.

Local Community Action

There is already evidence from work in Edinburgh that community action can play an important part in staving off crises. Briefly, this has been achieved by the establishment of a multi-disciplinary unit in an area where social malaise is at its highest. The unit operates with a team which includes every sub-speciality of social work, both voluntary and statutory, and includes the Citizens' Advice Bureau. It also includes representatives of the Ministries of Social Security and of Employment and Productivity and also acts as a base for the activities of other city departments such as the Housing Department.

Besides giving support of the more traditional social work nature, this unit has experimented with a more direct attack on the effects of poverty on these none-too-well integrated people. With the passing of the Children and Young Persons Act in 1963, provision was made for city children's departments to meet family crises with cash awards if such were seen to be necessary. Recent social work legislation in Scotland has widened the money-giving powers of local authorities. In most cities this facility is used in a fairly piecemeal manner, awards being made on the basis of individual assessments of merit by individual social workers. By utilizing this cash provision in a calculatedly more liberal fashion there have been dramatic reductions in the rates for eviction and for children being taken into care, two of the indices which featured in our ecological study. It has not been the aim of the unit to demoralize their clients by offering largesse—the aim has been to stem the crisis and thus buy time for real social work at an intensive level to be undertaken.

Alongside this "patching" policy there is another one which is aimed to stimulate community pride, having at its core citizens who, living in the area, are an integral part of the area. From this group real social action has been generated and it has produced so many positive, practical plans for the area that the civic authorities can no longer regard the area as being for ever beyond the pale. Briefly, the activities to which we refer include many of the functions of "the good neighbour", but even in this respect they have taken the novel step of fostering this neighbourliness by encouraging the more integrated to move towards the less integrated and to act as their alarm signals.

Poor Parent–Child Relationships

In Chapter 4 it was demonstrated that in many cases of suicidal behaviour there are histories of poor parent–child relationships, and it was suggested that this may account for the generally inadequate personalities which are seen in this group, especially in those who repeat. But it was also shown that as children our patients were already presenting to various social agencies; they were being taken into care, seen by the prevention of cruelty workers, seen by the juvenile courts, seen by education welfare officers, and, of course, by teachers. Where these agencies act independently there is too often a multiplicity of superficial contacts. A unit such as we have described acts as a clearing house for these various agencies and facilitates more effective intervention on a long-term basis. Fortunately, this experimental unit has taken the precaution of gathering data in a systematic way so that its effectiveness can be assessed from time to time. Its long-term task is not to tackle the problem of suicidal behaviour *per se* but rather to create a sense of "belonging" for the residents which, hope-fully, will effect a change in the all-too-common response to stress—attempted suicide. If our theory that good personal relationships can minimize the effects of stress is valid, then primary prevention must be aimed at the creation of such relationships, especially within family units.

In this book it has been shown that persons who attempt suicide are characterized by social and psychological deficits which pose severe problems for those who would treat them. Treatment is not impossible, however, but it cannot be cheap either in terms of money or professional and lay human investment. Clearly this behaviour is not a psychiatric syndrome although it has many associations with mental illness. It is a manifestation of a process which begins in early childhood and is socially nursed and channelled into a variety of behaviours, all of which are seen as deviant.

The authors have tried, however poorly, to help the reader to understand better the presenting symptom of social malaise towards suicidal behaviour. It is hoped, however, that they have indicated clearly that preventative work must be done with the whole person and with his social milieu rather than with any single symptom.

Bibliography

For the reader who wishes to pursue the study of suicidal behaviour and its prevention, the bibliography by Farberow is a key work of reference. It appears in the following list of readings, which we think make a major contribution to the understanding of attempted suicide as a social and psychological problem. Most of these general references are concerned with suicidal behaviour in a direct way; a few others are less restricted in content.

Following the general list is one of more specialized interest giving references to specific chapters of the book. This list will be of interest to those who wish to explore in greater depth some of the points we have raised.

General References

Burt, C. (1944) *The Young Delinquent*, 4th edn., University of London Press, Bickley.

Dahlgren, K. G. (1945) *On Suicide and Attempted Suicide*, Lundstedt, Lund.

Dublin, L. I. (1963) *Suicide: A Sociological and Statistical Study*, Ronald Press, New York.

Durkheim, E. (1897) *Le Suicide*, Libraire Félix Alcon, Paris.

Farberow, N. L. (1969) *Bibliography on Suicide and Suicide Prevention*, NIMH, Chevy Chase, Maryland.

Farberow, N. L. and Shneidman, E. S. (1961) *The Cry for Help*, McGraw-Hill, New York.

Foulds, G. A. (1965) *Personality and Personal Illness*, Tavistock, London.

Hollingshead, A. B. and Redlich, F. C. (1958) *Social Class and Mental Illness— A Community Study*, John Wiley, New York.

McCulloch, J. W. (1971) Social aspects of acute barbiturate poisoning, in *Acute Barbiturate Poisoning* (ed. H. Matthew), Excerpta Medica, Amsterdam.

McDavid, J. W. and Harari, H. (1968) *Social Psychology*, Harper, New York.

Menninger, K. A. (1938) *Man Against Himself*, Harcourt, Bruce & World, New York.

Munro, A. and McCulloch, J. W. (1969) Suicide and attempted suicide, chapter in *Psychiatry for Social Workers*, Pergamon Press, Oxford.

Ryle, A. (1967) *Neurosis in the Ordinary Family*, Tavistock, London.

SHNEIDMAN, E. S. (1964) Suicide, sleep and death: some possible interrelation among cessation, interruptions and continuous phenomena, *J. Consult. Psychol.* **28**, 95.

STENGEL, E. (1964) *Suicide and Attempted Suicide*, Penguin Books, Harmondsworth.

TAYLOR, LORD, and CHAVE, S. (1964) *Mental Health and Environment*, Longmans, London.

References of Specialized Interest

AINSWORTH, D. (1962) The effects of maternal deprivation, a review of findings and controversy in the context of research strategy, in *Deprivation of Maternal Care: A Reassessment*, WHO, Geneva.

AINSWORTH, D. (1965) Further research into the adverse effects of maternal deprivation, Part III, *Child Care and the Growth of Love*, 2nd edn. (ed. J. Bowlby), Pelican, Harmondsworth.

AITKEN, R. C. B., BUGLASS, D. and KREITMAN, N. (1969) The changing pattern of attempted suicide in Edinburgh 1962–7, *Br. J. prev. soc. Med.* **23** (2) 111.

ANNESLEY, P. T. (1961) Psychiatric illness in adolescents: presentation and prognosis, *J. ment. Sci.* **107**, 268.

ARESENIAN, S. M. (1943) Young children in an insecure situation, *J. abnorm. soc. Psychol.* **38**, 225.

BALSER, B. H. and MASTERTON, J. T. (1959) Suicide in adolescents, *Am. J. Psychiat.* **116**, 400.

BATCHELOR, I. R. C. (1954) Psychopathic states and attempted suicide, *Br. J. Delinq.* **4**, 99.

BATCHELOR, I. R. C. (1954) Repeated suicidal attempts, *Br. J. med. Psychol.* **27**, 158.

BATCHELOR, I. R. C. and NAPIER, M. B. (1953) Broken homes among attempted suicides, *Br. J. Delinq.* **4**, 99.

BENEDICT, R. (1934) *Patterns of Culture*, Houghton Mifflin, Boston.

BOWLBY, J. (1940) The influence of early environment, *Int. J. Psycho-Anal.* **21**, 154.

BOWLBY, J. (1944) Forty-four juvenile thieves; their character and home life, *Int. J. Psycho-Anal.* **25**, 107.

BOWLBY, J. (1956) *Maternal Care and Mental Health*, WHO, Geneva.

BOWLBY, J. (1960) chapter in *Psychoanalytic Study of the Child*, International University Press, New York.

BOWLBY, J. (1961) Childhood mourning and its implications for psychiatry, *Am. J. Psychiat.* **118**, 6.

BOWLBY, J. (1965) *Child Care and the Growth of Love*, 2nd edn., Pelican, Harmondsworth.

BOWLBY, J. (1969) *Attachment and Loss*, vol. 1, *Attachment*, Hogarth Press, London.

BRIDGES, P. K. and KOLLER, K. M. (1966) Attempted suicides: a comparative study, *Comp. Psychiat.* **7**, 240.

BRITISH MEDICAL JOURNAL (1969) National Poisons Information Service, Fifth Annual Report for the year ended 31.12.68, *Br. med. J.* **3**, 408.

BROWN, F. (1961) Depression and childhood bereavement, *J. ment. Sci.* **107**, 754.

BRUHN, J. G. (1962) Broken homes among attempted suicides and psychiatric outpatients—a comparative study, *J. ment. Sci.* **108**, 772.

BRUHN, J. G. and McCULLOCH, W. (1962) Parental deprivation among attempted suicides, *Br. J. psychiat. soc. Wk.* **6**, 186.

BUGLASS, D. and McCULLOCH, J. W. (1970) Further suicidal behaviour: the development and validation of predictive scales, *Br. J. Psychiat.* **116**, 483, 491.

BURR, C. W. (1905) Insanity at puberty, *J. Am. med. Ass.* **2**, 36.

CAPLAN, G. (1964) *Principles of Preventive Psychiatry*, Tavistock, London.

CARSTAIRS, G. M. (1961) Characteristics of the suicide prone, *Proc. R. Soc. Med.* **54**, 262.

CARSTAIRS, G. M. (1963) *This Island Now*, Hogarth, London.

CARTER, A. B. (1942) The prognostic factors of adolescent psychoses, *J. ment. Sci.* **88**, 31.

CASLER, L. (1961) Maternal deprivation: a critical review of the literature, *Monogr. Soc. Res. Child. Dev.* **26**, 2.

CATTELL, R. B. (1957) *Personality and Motivation Structure and Measurement*, Harrap, London.

CATTELL, R. B. (1964) Psychological definition and measurement of anxiety, *J. Neuropsychiat.* **5**, 396.

CATTELL, R. B. (1965) *The Scientific Analysis of Personality*, Penguin, Harmondsworth.

CLARKE, A. D. B. and CLARKE, A. M. (1960) Some recent advances in the study of early deprivation, *J. Child Psychol. Psychiat.* **1**, 26.

CLAUSEN, J. and KOHN, M. (1954) The ecological approach in social psychiatry, *Am. J. Sociol.* **60**, 140.

COHEN, E., MOTTO, J. and SEIDEN, R. H. (1966) An instrument for evaluating suicide potential: a preliminary study, *Am. J. Psychiat.* **122**, 886.

COHEN, J. (1960) *Chance Skill and Luck*, Penguin, Harmondsworth.

CRANDELL, D. L. and DOHRENWEND, B. P. (1967) Social relations among psychiatric symptoms, organic illness and social class, *Am. J. Psychiat.* **123**, 1527.

DELANO, J. G. (1963) Psychiatric implications of the teenager's problems, *J. Am. med. Ass.* **184**, 539.

DORPAT, T. L., JACKSON, J. J. and RIPLEY, H. S. (1965) Broken homes and attempted and completed suicide, *Archs. gen. Psychiat.* **12**, 213.

DUNHAM, H. W. (1959) *Sociological Theory and Mental Disorder*, Wayne State University Press, Detroit.

EAST, W. N. (1913) On attempted suicide with an analysis of 1000 consecutive cases, *J. ment. Sci.* **59**, 428.

EBIE, J. C., HICKS, R. C., LYTHE, G. J. and SHORT, R. (1970) An integrated approach to a community's health and social problems, *Health Bulletin, Scottish Home and Health Department*, **28** (2) 35–41.

ERIKSON, E. H. (1960) The problems of ego identity, *Psychol. Issues* **1**, 101.

ETTLINGER, R. (1964) Suicide in a group of patients who had previously attempted suicide, *Acta psychiat. scand.* **40**, 363.

FAIGEL, H. C. (1966) Suicide among young persons: a review for its incidence and causes, and methods of its prevention, *Clin. Pediat.* **5**, 187–90.

FARBEROW, N. L. (1959) Validity and methodology in projective tests, *J. proj. Tech.* **23**, 282.

FARBEROW, N. L. (1960) Personality patterns of suicidal mental hospital patients, *Genet. psychol. Monogr.* **42**, 3.

FARIS, R. E. L. and DUNHAM, H. W. (1939) *Mental Disorders in Urban Areas,* University of Chicago Press, Chicago.

FERENCZI, S. (1929) The unwelcome child—his death instinct, *Int. J. Psycho-Anal.* **10**, 125.

FOULDS, G. A. (1967) Some differences between neurotics and character disorders, *Br. J. soc. clin. Psychol.* **6**, 52.

FOULDS, G. A. and HOPE, K. (1968) *Manual of the Symptom Sign Inventory,* University of London Press, London.

GARDENER, E. A., BAHN, A. K. and MACK, M. (1964) Suicide and psychiatric care in the ageing, *Archs. gen. Psychiat.* **10**, 547.

GAY, M. J. and TONGE, W. L. (1967) Late effects of loss of parents in childhood, *Br. J. Psychiat.* **113**, 753.

GESSELL, A. (1954) *The First Five Years of Life; A Guide to the Study of the Pre-school Child,* Methuen, London.

GIBBENS, T. C. N. (1961) *Trends in Juvenile Delinquency,* WHO, Geneva.

GLUECK, S. and GLUECK, E. (1950) *Unravelling Juvenile Delinquency,* Harvard University Press, Massachusetts.

GOLDFARB, W. (1955) Emotional and intellectual consequences of psychological deprivation in infancy: A Revaluation, in *Psychopathology of Childhood* (Hoch and Zubin, eds.), Grune & Stratton, London.

GREER, S. (1964) The relationship between parental loss and attempted suicide: a control study, *Br. J. Psychiat.* **110**, 698.

GREER, S. (1966) Parental loss and attempted suicide: a further report, *Br. J. Psychiat.* **112**, 465.

GREER, S. and GUNN, J. L. (1966) Attempted suicides from intact and broken parental homes, *Br. med. J.* **2**, 1355–7.

GUERRIN, R. F. and BORGATTA, E. F. (1965) Socio-economic and demographic correlates of tuberculosis incidence, *Milbank Mem. Fund. Quart.* **43**, 269.

HARE, E. H. and SHAW, G. K. (1965) *Mental Health in a New Housing Estate,* Oxford University Press, London.

HARRINGTON, J. A. and CROSS, J. W. (1959) Cases of attempted suicide admitted to a general hospital, *Br. med. J.* **2**, 463.

HENDERSON, A. S., McCULLOCH, J. W. and PHILIP, A. E. (1967) Survey of mental illness in adolescence, *Br. med. J.* **1**, 83.

HINKLE, L. E. and WOLFF, H. G. (1958) Ecologic investigations of the relationships between illness, life experiences and the social environment, *Ann. intern. Med.* **49**, 1373.

HMSO (1955) *Unsatisfactory Tenants,* 6th Report of the Housing Management Sub-Committee of the Central Housing Advisory Committee.

HORSLEY, S. (1965) The cost of preventive psychiatry, *Med. Officer*, **113**, 341.

HOVE, H. (1953) Fates of intercepted suicides: follow-up of 500 cases, *J. Am. med. Ass.* **152**, 1649.

JACOBS, J. and TEICHER, J. D. (1967) Broken homes and social isolation in attempted suicide of adolescents. *Int. J. soc. Psychiat.* **13** (2) 139–49.

JACOBZINER, H. (1960) Attempted suicide in children, *J. Paediat.* **56**, 519.

JACOBZINER, H. (1965) Attempted suicide in adolescence, *J. Am. med. Ass.* **191**, 7.

JAN-TAUSCH, J. (n.d.) Suicide of children 1960–3, New Jersey public school students, *Trenton NJ State of NJ Dept. Educ.*

JEFFREYS, M. (1965) *An Anatomy of Social Welfare Services*, Michael Joseph, London.

KAY, M. (1968) Personality and adjustment problems of students in training for teaching: a contribution to development psychology, unpublished PhD thesis, University of Leicester.

KEMP, R. (1957) Morbidity and social class, *Lancet* **1**, 1316.

KESSEL, N. (1965) Self-poisoning, *Br. med. J.* **2**, 1265, 1336.

KESSEL, N. (1966) The respectability of self-poisoning and the fashion of survival, *J. psychosom. Res.* **10**, 29.

KESSEL, N. and GROSSMAN, G. (1961) Suicide in alcoholics, *Br. med. J.* **2**, 1671.

KESSEL, N. and LEE, E. McC. (1962) Attempted suicide in Edinburgh, *Scot. med. J.* **7**, 130.

KESSEL, N., McCULLOCH, W. and SIMPSON, E. (1963) Psychiatric service in a centre for the treatment of poisoning, *Br. med. J.* **2**, 985.

KESSEL, N. and McCULLOCH, W. (1966) Repeated acts of self-poisoning and self-injury, *Proc. R. Soc. Med.* **59**, 89.

KREITMAN, N. (1961) The reliability of psychiatric diagnosis, *J. ment. Sci.* **107**, 876.

KREITMAN, N., SMITH, P. and TAN, E. (1969) Attempted suicide in social networks, *Br. J. prev. soc. Med.* **23**, 116.

LEBOVICI, S. (1962) The concept of maternal deprivation: a review of research, in *Deprivation of Maternal Care: a Reassessment*, WHO, Geneva.

LEESE, S. M. (1969) Suicide behaviour in twenty adolescents. *Br. J. Psychiat.* **115**, 479–80.

LOWLER, R. H., NAKIELRY, W. and WRIGHT, N. (1963) Juvenile suicide attempts, *Can. Med. Ass. J.* **89**, 751.

McBOYLE REPORT (1963) *Prevention of Neglect of Children (Scotland)*, HMSO.

McCARTHY, P. D. and WALSH, D. (1966) Suicide in Dublin, *Br. med. J.* **1**, 1393.

McCORD, W. and McCORD, J. (1964) *The Psychopath*, Van Nostrand, Princeton, NJ.

McCULLOCH, J. W. (1965) The social consequences of acts of deliberate self-poisoning or self-injury, unpublished MSc dissertation, University of Edinburgh.

McCULLOCH, J. W., HENDERSON, A. S. and PHILIP, A. E. (1966) Psychiatric illness in Edinburgh teenagers, *Scot. med. J.* **11**, 277.

McCULLOCH, J. W. and PHILIP, A. E. (1967) Social variables in attempted suicide, *Acta psychiat. scand.* **43**, 341.

McCulloch, J. W. and Philip, A. E. (1967) Social factors associated with attempted suicide: a review of the literature, *Br. J. psychiat. soc. Wk.* **9**, 30.

McCulloch, J. W., Philip, A. E. and Carstairs, G. M. (1967) The ecology of suicidal behaviour, *Br. J. Psychiat.* **113**, 313.

McCulloch, J. W. and Philip, A. E. (1970) The social prognosis of persons who attempt suicide, *Soc. Psychiat.* **5**, 177.

McQuitty, L. L. (1957) Elementary linkage analysis for isolating orthogonal and oblique types and typal relevancies, *Educ. psychol. Measur.* **17**, 207.

Madow, L. and Hardy, S. E. (1947) Incidence and analysis of the broken family in the background of neurosis, *Am. J. Orthopsychiat.* **17**, 521.

Mannheim, K. and Wilkins, L. (1956) *Prediction Method in Relation to Borstal Training*, HMSO, London.

Mayer-Gross, W., Slater, E. and Roth, M. (1960), *Clinical Psychiatry*, Cassell, London.

Munro, A. (1969) The theoretical importance of parental deprivation in the aetiology of psychiatric illness, *Appl. soc. Studies* **1**, 81.

Neuringer, C. (1965) The Rorschach test as a device for the identification, prediction, and understanding of suicidal ideation and behaviour, *J. Project. Tech. Personal. Assess.* **29** (1) 71–82.

Parkin, D. and Stengel, E. (1965) Incidence of suicidal attempts in an urban community, *Br. med. J.* **2**, 133.

Philip, A. E. (1968) Personality factors involved in suicidal behaviour, unpublished PhD thesis, University of Edinburgh.

Philip, A. E. (1969a) The development and use of the hostility and direction of hostility questionnaire, *J. psychosom. Res.* **13**, 283.

Philip, A. E. and McCulloch, J. W. (1966) The use of social indices in psychiatric epidemiology, *Br. J. prev. soc. Med.* **20**, 122.

Philip, A. E. and McCulloch, J. W. (1967) Social pathology and personality in attempted suicide, *Br. J. Psychiat.* **133**, 1405.

Philip, A. E. and McCulloch, J. W. (1968) Personal construct theory and social work practice, *Br. J. soc. clin. Psychol.* **7**, 115.

Philip, A. E. and McCulloch, J. W. (1968) Some psychological features of persons who have attempted suicide, *Br. J. Psychiat.* **114**, 1299.

Philip, A. E. and McCulloch, J. W. (1970) Test–retest characteristics of a group of attempted suicide patients, *J. consult. clin. Psychol.* **34**, 144.

Power, M. J. (1965) An attempt to identify at first appearance before the courts those at risk of becoming persistent offenders, *Proc. R. Soc. Med.* **58**, 704.

Robins, E., Schmidt, E. H. and O'Neal, P. (1957) Some interrelations of social factors and clinical diagnoses in attempted suicide, a study of 109 patients, *Am. J. Psychiat.* **114**, 221.

Sainsbury, P. (1955) *Suicide in London*, Chapman & Hall, London.

Sainsbury, P. and Barraclough, B. (1968) Difference between suicide rates, *Nature* **220**, 1252.

SCHNEIDER, E. V. (1953) Sociological concepts and psychiatric research, chapter in *Interrelations between the Social Environment and Psychiatric Disorders*, Millbank Memorial Fund, New York.

SCHRUT, A. (1964) Suicidal adolescents and children, *J. Am. med. Ass.* **188**, 1103–7.

SCLARE, A. E. and HAMILTON, C. M. (1963) Attempted suicide in Glasgow, *Br. J. Psychiat.* **109**, 609.

SCOTTISH HOME and HEALTH DEPARTMENT (1964) *Children and Young Persons, Scotland* (1964), HMSO, Edinburgh.

SEIDEN, R. H. (1966) Campus tragedy: a study of student suicide, *J. abnormal Psychol.* **71** (6) 389–99.

SHNEIDMAN, E. S. and FARBEROW, N. L. (1960) A socio-psychological investigation of suicide, chapter in *Perspectives in Personality Research* (eds. H. P. David and J. S. Brengelmann), Springer, New York.

SHORT, R. and McCULLOCH, J. W. (1968) Health, welfare, and advice centre: an experiment in a multi-disciplinary approach to the prevention of social and medico-psychological problems, *Case Conference* **15** (3) 107.

STENGEL, E. and COOK, N. (1958) *Attempted Suicide: Its Social Significance and Effects*, Oxford University Press, London.

STENGEL, E. and COOK, G. (1961) Contrasting suicide rates in industrial communities, *J. ment. Sci.* **107**, 1011.

STOTT, D. H. (1960) Delinquency, maladjustment, and unfavourable ecology, *Br. J. Psychol.* **51**, 157.

TEICHER, J. D. (1947) A study in attempted suicide, *J. nerv. ment. Dis.* **105**, 283.

THOMPSON, W. R. (1955) Early environment—its importance for later behaviour, chapter in *Psychopathology of Childhood* (Hoch and Zubin, eds.), Grune & Stratton, London.

TOOLAN, J. M. (1962) Suicide and suicidal attempts in children and adolescents, *Am. J. Psychiat.* **118**, 719.

TUCKMAN, J. and YOUNGMAN, W. F. (1963) Suicide risk among persons attempting suicide, *Publ. Hlth. Rep.* **78**, 585.

TUCKMAN, J. and YOUNGMAN, W. F. (1964) Attempted suicide and family dis-organisation, *J. genet. Psychol.* **105**, 187.

US DEPARTMENT OF HEALTH, EDUCATION AND WELFARE (1965) *Changes in Mortality Trends England and Wales 1931–1961*, US Public Health Service, Washington.

VINODA, K. S. (1964) A study of personality characteristics of attempted suicides, unpublished PhD thesis, University of London.

VINODA, K. S. (1966) Personality characteristics of attempted suicide, *Br. J. Psychiat.* **112**, 1143.

WALSH, D. and McCARTHY, P. D. (1965) Suicide in Dublin's elderly, *Acta psychiat. scand.* **41**, 227.

WASSERMYER, M. (1913) Über Selbstmord, *Arch. f. Psychiar.* **50**, 255.

WHITLOCK, F. A. and SHAPIRA, K. (1967) Attempted suicide in Newcastle-upon-Tyne, *Br. J. Psychiat.* **113**, 423.

WILKINS, L. T. (1963) Juvenile delinquency: a critical review of research and theory, *Educ. Res.* **5**, 104.

WORLD HEALTH ORGANIZATION (1968) *Prevention of Suicide*, Public Health Paper No. 35, Geneva.

ZILBOORG, G. (1936) Suicide among civilised and primitive races, *Am. J. Psychiat.* **92**, 1347–69.

ZMUC, M. (1968) Alcohol and suicide, *Alcoholism* **4**, 1.

Index

119

fSB